The Sermon Slot

THE SERMON SLOT

□ *Ideas for all-age worship*

YEAR 2

SHARON J. SWAIN

Illustrated by Taffy Davies

This book is dedicated to Rev. Faith Cully

First published in Great Britain 1993
Society for Promoting Christian Knowledge
Holy Trinity Church
Marylebone Road
London NW1 4DU

British Library Cataloguing-in-Publication Data
A catalogue record for this book is available from the British Library

ISBN 0-281-04696-4

Typeset by Latimer Trend, Plymouth
Printed in Great Britain by
The Cromwell Press, Melksham, Wiltshire

Contents

Introduction

The Sermon Slot: Year 2, is the second of two books based on the church's two-year cyle of readings. It aims to give those who are responsible for organizing all-age services some suggestions for incorporating them into the traditional 'sermon slot'.

The book allows for wide varieties of situations, and encourages leaders to tailor the suggestions to suit their own individual needs. Although the ideas are based on themes and readings as laid out in the Lectionary, this is not first and foremost a book about Bible study, but rather a compendium of practical suggestions to help the leader expound more fully the word of God.

☐ *The family service*

The 'family' or 'all-age' service reminds us that we are all on a journey of pilgrimage together. Children and adults need each other to progress along the path, and to learn and worship apart can hinder their progress.

The traditional family service must no longer be a children's service, or indeed a time when the church pays lip service to its children. The family service, whether it is eucharistic or not, must take account of all ages in the church.

The organizer of the family service faces a challenge to occupy the adult's mind (and often, though not always, their maturer understanding of the faith), as well as the children's desire to worship with their whole body.

The Sermon Slot gives ideas for those faced with the challenges of conducting all-age services. It uses the traditional teaching point of the service to allow congregations to stop and look at the message of Jesus Christ and at their response.

The book is not intended to be exclusive to parish churches. Many denominations use the same cycle of readings and, for all, the challenges of the all-age service are the same.

☐ *The all-age service*

For those who wish to get the most out of this book the following suggestions might be helpful:

- All-age services need a *team* of people to organize them. Do not expect the vicar or minister to do it all.
- All-age services need *advance planning* and *prayer*. Think and plan at least four or five weeks ahead to get the best out of the service.
- All-age services must be *flexible*. Anything can – and often

does – happen when those who take the service are using modern methods of education. You may also need to tailor the instructions to suit your circumstances, and double the number of groups or dispense with some. But with the Holy Spirit's help, and good planning, even difficulties can be turned to your benefit.

- All-age services are for *everyone*. You cannot always keep the two-year-old occupied, or indeed the ninety-year-old, but there should be something for each in the service.
- All-age services are for *equals*. Never talk down to children or new adults in church. They may know more than you, or be spiritual giants. Equally, don't expect those who have been worshipping for fifty years to know all the answers, for they won't. In the all-age service all are equals!
- All-age services need the *good will* of some people. If flak occurs don't give in, but do question whether you went too fast at first. Don't threaten anyone by asking them direct questions, or by making them take part. Take things slowly and don't try to change everything overnight.
- All-age services are *fun*. Learning about God can be fun as well as instructive. So enjoy yourself.

Abbreviations
CP   *Come and Praise*. BBC Radio for schools. BBC Books.
JP   *Junior Praise*. Peter J. Horrobin and Greg Leavers. Marshall Pickering 1986.
MP   *Mission Praise*. Peter J. Horrobin and Greg Leavers, eds. Marshal Pickering 1990.
SGP *Songs of God's People*. Oxford University Press 1988.
WS   *Worship Song Book*. Kingsway 1989.

9th SUNDAY BEFORE CHRISTMAS

 The Creation
Jesus says that we can be born again. What changes might this
bring to our lives, and where could we start?

John 3.1–8

Copies of the form for all the congregation.
Pencils.
Some wigs if desired, and a mirror.

☐ *Introduction*
Discuss with the congregation what it would be like to choose a
new appearance. What would they like to change about
themselves? Would they choose to have different hair colour or
eyes or height? Would they wish to look like someone else? Or
would they prefer to stay as they are?

Optional | If appropriate, get hold of some wigs and encourage some of the
congregation to change their hair style and colouring by trying
them on.

☐ *If I were born again*
Before the service, create sufficient copies of the form shown
below for each member of the congregation.
   Give out the forms, together with pencils, and encourage
everyone to fill in the front of the form.

	(Front of Form)	(Back of Form)
	If I were born again I would like to change my	*If I were born again* I would like to make the following changes to my character
height	. . . .	. . . .
colour of eyes	. . . .	. . . .
colour of hair	. . . .	. . . .
anything else	. . . .	. . . .

Allow time for discussion and encourage young children to work with adults or teenagers.

When everyone has completed the front of the form encourage them to talk to a neighbour about what changes they might wish to make to their personality. For instance, would they like to have greater patience, be more loving, or refrain from losing their temper? If they were given the chance to start again, what changes would they make to their character?

After a few moments ask everyone to use the *reverse* side of their form to note the changes they would like to make to their characters. Note that these will be completely anonymous!

Younger children could be encouraged to put down things like 'sharing toys' or 'being nice to my brother'.

☐   *Comment*
Refer to the Gospel reading (John 3.1–8) for the day. Jesus says we can be born again through loving God and allowing the Holy Spirit to work in our lives. The changes that will occur in our lives will be as great as though we were born again. It will be as if we were born with different coloured hair, or eyes, or body.

Remind the congregation of the changes that they would like to see in themselves. With God's help they can change and be born again into the new kind of person that God wishes them to be.

☐   *Conclusion*
Close this part of the service with a moment of silence, to allow the congregation to reflect upon the changes they wish to make in their lives.

If appropriate the forms can be collected in and offered at the altar. They should be carefully disposed of to ensure confidentiality.

2

8th SUNDAY BEFORE CHRISTMAS

The Fall
An illustrated talk demonstrates graphically our responsibility for the kind of person we become. With God's help, however, the mess of our lives can be cleaned up!

Genesis 3.1–15   John 3.13–21

> An overhead projector or board and paper, and felt-tip pens.
> A sheet of A4 white paper.
> An adult or child to draw a picture on the screwed-up piece of paper.
> A sheet of A4 white paper covered with black scribble.
> A paper plane made from white paper.
> An attractive black and white picture.
> Paper and pencils. '
> Container for burning confessions.
> Matches.
> Sugar-paper and large felt-tip pen if desired.

□   *Introduction*
Remind the congregation that God made the world, and that everything he made in this act of creation was made perfect, including human beings. However we have spoiled God's great creation.

Discuss with the congregation ways in which we have ruined God's creation. List these, if desired, on an overhead projector or board and paper. For example:

- polluted the sea;
- poisoned the atmosphere;
- killed animals to extinction;
- destroyed the perfect human beings God made.

□   *Game*
Conduct a game of 'Chinese whispers' to show the way that perfection can become distorted. Whisper messages to two people at the front of the church and ask them to pass the messages on until they reach those at the back of the church. By this time the two messages should be hopelessly distorted. Gather them in and compare to the original versions.

3

☐ *Comment*

Refer to the Old Testament reading (Genesis 3.1–15). This is another way of thinking about the Fall. God made Adam and Eve perfect, but he also gave them free will and they chose to disobey him. Men and women became separated from God because of their sin.

Refer to the Gospel reading (John 3.13–21). God out of his goodness created a plan to bring us back into loving contact with him again.

☐ *Talk: The piece of paper*

Take a blank piece of white paper and ask the congregation to imagine that we are all like this sheet of paper. We were made perfect, but we have destroyed God's perfection.

Crush the paper violently and throw it at a member of the congregation who has been previously primed to flatten out the sheet and draw an interesting picture on it by the end of the talk.

Continue by reminding everyone of how selfish, greedy and unloving humans can be. Use a paper plane as an example of this. An aeroplane is a beautiful thing, but it can be used for war as well as going on holiday! We too are lovely creatures but the seeds of violence are always within us. Throw the paper plane towards the congregation.

Now show the congregation the scribbled piece of paper. The pure white sheet of paper has been ruined. We too make a mess of our lives. We mean to go the way God wants but somehow things go wrong, and the picture becomes a mess. Screw the piece of paper up and throw it away.

Finally add that even though we destroy ourselves and ruin the original perfection, God will forgive us. Refer to the Gospel reading (John 3.13–21). Jesus says that God so loves us that he gave his only Son, that whoever believes in him should have eternal life. We can make our peace with God, and out of the mess of our lives God will help us to start again.

☐ *Conclusion*

Ask the person who has created a drawing on the screwed-up piece of paper to show it to the congregation. Comment that from the rubbish that was thrown away something good has emerged. God allows us to start again and to create something good from the mess we have made (even though we fail him again and again). When we ask God's forgiveness he rescues us to start again.

Encourage the congregation to write down their confessions. Younger children can be helped by adults. Then ask everyone to fold up the pieces of paper.

Collect these and burn in a suitable container during the service. If necessary, do this outside. No words of absolution should be said.

Note: If you are thinking of using the service for the 7th Sunday before Christmas, you will need to ask three or four adults and children to bring some 'precious possessions' to church the following week.

7th SUNDAY BEFORE CHRISTMAS

The election of God's people: Abraham
Abraham was willing to give God the most precious thing in his life – his son Isaac – because of his faith. The theme of Faith is explored by looking at what is precious to us, today.

Genesis 22.1–18   James 2.14–24

The Old Testament lesson should be read with a variety of different voices. Use the Dramatized Bible if possible.

Paper and pencils if desired.
Three or four adults and children and their precious possessions.
Copy of the litany and two readers.

☐ *Introduction*

Ask the congregation to think of things that are precious to them. Do not suggest what is precious, but ask them to play a game of 'If my house were on fire, I would save . . .'. Instruct them to rescue three things from their house. What would they decide to save from the fire?

Allow small children to work with parents or adults, but otherwise encourage everyone to keep their thoughts to themselves. You might wish the choices to be written down on slips of paper and handed in to be read anonymously, or you could ask different people to offer their choices aloud.

Many people will choose to save inanimate objects like photograph albums, wedding presents or a teddy, and forget to save their children, or granny, or the dog. Read out a number of the choices before commenting on this!

☐ *Talk: Precious possessions*

Continue by inviting three or four previously primed adults and children to join you, bringing their most precious possessions with them. Question each (or ask them to give a short talk) as to why the object in question is their most precious possession.

Try to ensure that your volunteers bring a variety of precious items and encourage at least one to say that their most precious possession is a member of their family.

Optional: Charity sale Initiate a collection of 'precious gifts' during this service, and hold a sale or auction before Christmas in aid of a project of your choosing.

☐ *Conclusion*

Refer to the theme of Faith and to the Old Testament reading

(Genesis 22.1–18). Abraham had such faith in God that he was able to put his precious son Isaac at risk. God had told Abraham that he was to be the father of millions, yet here he was about to kill his only son. Still Abraham had faith in God that things would be all right.

FAITH IS ....

For us, having faith is like being able to give up our most precious possessions because God asks this of us, and yet we know they will be safe. It is trusting God, despite ourselves and our rational mind.

But, it is not enough to *say* we have faith, we must *show* we have faith by our actions. We are living by faith when we give away our money (or our toys) to help those in need. We are living by faith when we give up our well-paid job to work for those who need our help. We are living by faith when we set aside time to pray for those in need. Maybe God is calling us to show that we have faith in him today.

 Continue the idea of precious items by creating a litany that reflects the two sides of affluence and need. Use two voices, with the refrain from the congregation occurring every other bidding:

> *Voice 1*: Lord, we thank you for our homes; for food and clean water, for warmth and the love of family and friends.
> *Voice 2*: Help us to create a better world: to work for those who have nowhere to live, for those who will receive no food this day, and those who have no one to love them. Lord, in your mercy.
> *All*: Hear our prayer.
>
> *Voice 1*: Lord, we thank you for. . . .

Continue the litany by looking at the relative peace of our own homes and society (if appropriate) against the need for peace elsewhere; and at health over against sickness and death.

6th SUNDAY BEFORE CHRISTMAS

The promise of redemption: Moses
The theme of covenants is explored by looking at the covenant made between God and Moses. The congregation are then encouraged to make their own covenants with God.

Exodus 6.2–8

> Six people to illustrate, using simple sketches, the nature of a covenant.
> Bibles for the congregation, if desired.
> A covenant form for each member of the congregation.
> Pencils.
> Copies of the Methodist covenant prayer or baptismal promises on an overhead projector transparency.

☐ *Introduction: Covenant sketches*
Produce some short sketches with the help of adults and children from the congregation. They could be previously rehearsed, but this is not essential as long as each actor knows the plot.

The sketches should all illustrate a covenant or a two-way agreement between different people.

Examples
1. A parent and child agree that if the child keeps their room tidy they will receive a certain amount of pocket money.

2. A husband and wife agree that if one will do the cooking, the other will do the cleaning.

Make sure that the two-way nature of the covenant is stressed – that each party to the covenant offers something.

☐ *Comment and Bible study*

Remind the congregation that God made covenants with a number of people. Look at the Old Testament reading (Exodus 6.2–8). Here we see God making a covenant with the Jewish people to give them the land of Canaan. In return the Israelites will acknowledge him as their God.

If sufficient Bibles are available ask everyone to look up first the covenant made with Noah (Genesis 9.8–17), and then the covenant made with Abram (Genesis 15.18–21).

Refer to the new covenant which was made with Jesus (Mark 14.24) and look up the reading if desired.

Jesus promises to repair the relationship between ourselves and God. He offers forgiveness of sin and eternal life. Our part in the agreement is to have faith in him.

☐ *Renewing our covenant with God*

Conclude by inviting the congregation to renew their covenant with God (or to create a totally new covenant with him), and hand out forms created for the purpose.

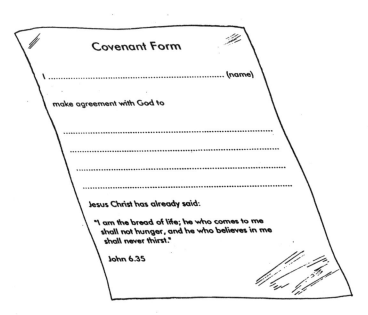

You may need to discuss the kind of covenant people may wish to make with God; for example, 'I promise to be nice to . . .' or 'read my Bible', etc. Each person should be encouraged to make out their own agreement with God. Families could make out joint covenants.

Optional
- Churches operating stewardship campaigns, or reviewing offertory schemes, may wish to renew their monetary covenants at this service.
- Where appropriate, invite members to come forward and make their covenant with God in a much more symbolic or public way.
- Emphasis could be laid on an annual Gift Day.

☐ *Conclusion*
The covenant forms could be put into named envelopes and then collected in to be offered at the altar with a suitable prayer. Make sure that they are duly returned to each person six months or a year later for people to reflect on whether the covenants have been kept.

Use the covenant prayer from the Methodist covenant service. If possible put the words on an over-head projector so that everyone can say them.

Alternatively, if you are not going to renew baptismal promises later in the year these could be included here.

5th SUNDAY BEFORE CHRISTMAS

The Remnant of Israel
God's call to us on 'Stir up Sunday' is explored by looking at his involvement in our lives. The congregation are called to rethink their commitment to God.

Isaiah 10.20–23   Romans 9.19–28

Paper and pens for all the congregation.
A large example of a 'lifeline' to show the congregation.
Candles or a cross to act as a focal point.
Copy of the litany.

☐ *Introduction*

Remind the congregation that today is often called 'Stir up
Sunday' because of the opening words of the collect for the day,
'Stir up, O Lord, the wills of your faithful people.' We are called
to 'stir ourselves' spiritually in this time before Christmas.

The readings (Isaiah 10.20–23 and Romans 9.19–28) remind us
that God has called us to follow his way, but that only a small
number of those who are called choose to listen to him.

Today is the time to

STOP, LISTEN and REFLECT.

☐ *Lifelines*

Give out pencils and paper, and ask the congregation to draw
their lifelines, putting in the most important events and dates of
their lives and indicating if they are 'high' or 'low' points in their
lives.

You might wish to create a fictional lifeline for everyone to see
on an over-head projector or board.

Encourage younger children to talk the idea over with parents
or friends before creating a small-scale version.

☐ *Example of a lifeline*

1955	1959	1960	1963	1975	1981	Present

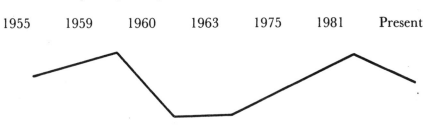

Sister born	Started school	Friend died	Left home	Married	Changed jobs

Allow a specific time for this task so that the second part of the
activity, below, can also be completed.

☐ *Spiritual lifeline*

When everyone has finished their lifeline, ask them to go back
over it and add a spiritual lifeline showing the highs and lows of
their spiritual life. These are the times when God felt near to
them, and the times when they seemed to be struggling with their
faith. Perhaps baptism or confirmation were highs, a death in the
family might be a low (or a high), and a walk out in the
countryside could be a high. These spiritual highs and lows might
be the opposite or the same as those of their lifeline.

11

Example

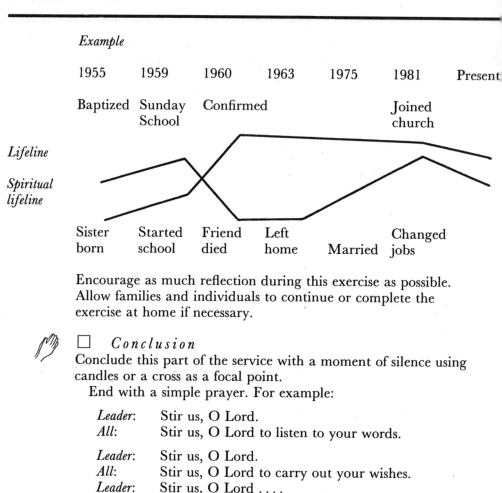

| 1955 | 1959 | 1960 | 1963 | 1975 | 1981 | Present |

Baptized Sunday   Confirmed   Joined
          School   church

Lifeline

*Spiritual
lifeline*

Sister   Started   Friend   Left   Changed
born   school   died   home   Married   jobs

Encourage as much reflection during this exercise as possible.
Allow families and individuals to continue or complete the
exercise at home if necessary.

 ☐ *Conclusion*

Conclude this part of the service with a moment of silence using
candles or a cross as a focal point.

End with a simple prayer. For example:

Leader: Stir us, O Lord.
All: Stir us, O Lord to listen to your words.

Leader: Stir us, O Lord.
All: Stir us, O Lord to carry out your wishes.
Leader: Stir us, O Lord . . . .

1st SUNDAY IN ADVENT

The Advent hope

The congregation are encouraged to review their Christian
response to the world, and in doing so to shake themselves out of
any feeling of complacency.

Isaiah 51.4–11   Matthew 25.31–end (a dramatized reading
would be appropriate)

Overhead projector or board and paper, and felt-tip pens.
A list of the tasks and suggested projects for each group.

☐ *Introduction*
Remind the congregation that this is the first Sunday in Advent,
and that the theme for the day is 'The Advent hope'. The sense
of urgency that God's kingdom is coming continues, and there is a
real need to give up our bad ways and follow the commands of
our Lord Jesus for the hope that he holds out.

Comment that the two readings (Isaiah 51.4–11 and Matthew
25.31–end) remind us that we shall be held to account for our
actions in this world. To ignore the needs of the world will be to
ignore Jesus.

With only four weeks to Christmas, now is the time to think
and act, for it may be too late to change our ways if we leave it
to another day.

☐ *Discussion: Helping others*
As a congregation, spend a few moments looking at how your
church and the wider church community helps those people
mentioned in the Gospel reading—the hungry, the thirsty, the
stranger, the naked and the sick. Be honest with yourselves!

☐ *Groupwork*
After some general discussion, create small groups giving each
group a task. Use an overhead projector or large board to display
plans or suggestions as they come in. Keep a note of decisions
made by each group and arrange for reports about any projects
set up to be returned at the service held on the 1st Sunday after
Epiphany.

Give each group the following instructions:

Project Hope
Today you are invited to play 'Project Hope'. Your group
project will bring help to someone in need.

● Start by choosing one of these five categories:

the hungry
the thirsty
the stranger
the naked
the sick.

● Decide whether you wish to help people overseas, or in your
own country (nationally or locally).

- Choose whether to raise money or materials, or to become actively involved in running a project.
- Make plans to carry out your 'Project Hope' in the next few weeks.
- Report back on the 1st Sunday after Epiphany with the results of your project.

Encourage each group to make plans that include children and young adults, and stress that projects may be small or large. They should suit all circumstances. The most important thing is that all the projects are actually carried out.

You may wish to ensure a spread of the different categories, so that not every group chooses, for instance, 'the sick'.

Suggested projects
- Collect good quality merchandise for a charity shop, or for the WRVS.
- Offer help to a Christmas Shelter programme, in terms of money or personnel.
- Adopt a local old folks' home, and find out what can be done to help.
- Raise money for water programmes in Third World countries.
- Visit sick or lonely people.
- Offer to clean or paint an elderly person's house, or tidy up the garden.
- Invite someone living alone to stay over Christmas.

☐ *Conclusion*
Re-read the words from St Matthew's Gospel: 'When I was hungry, you gave me food, you visited me.'

Allow a moment's silent prayer.

2nd SUNDAY IN ADVENT
(Bible Sunday)

The Word of God in the Old Testament
The congregation are encouraged to examine the Old Testament
for prophetic evidence to the coming of Jesus which is then
transferred to pictorial form.

Luke 4.14–21   Romans 15.4–13

> Sufficient Bibles for each group.
> A Jesse Tree made from branches stuck in a pot filled with
> earth.
> Coloured card, scissors, pencils and thread to hang the
> symbols on the tree.

☐ *Introduction*
Inform the congregation that today is Bible Sunday. Comment
that we are going to spend some time looking at the Old
Testament for evidence of God's work in the world as shown in
the different characters who prefigure the coming of Jesus.

Refer to the New Testament lesson (Romans 15.4–13) and the
Gospel reading (Luke 4.14–21) if desired. St Paul says that the
root of Jesse will flower so that from it will come the one who is
to govern the Gentiles. While Jesus uses Isaiah's words to make
this claim about himself, here his emphasis is on releasing
prisoners and protecting the poor.

It is important at this time of the year to remind ourselves
about all those who were Jesus' ancestors, and who point forward
to the coming of the Messiah.

☐ *Groupwork: Choosing a Bible story*
Create *small* groups of mixed ages and allocate at least one Bible
to each group. Ask the groups to act together and collectively to
choose a favourite story concerning a person from the Old
Testament. Look up the story and read it from the Bible.

If the groups find it difficult to decide on one story, more could
be chosen. However, try to encourage them to work together and
if possible to cover the whole period between Adam and Jesus (to
include John the Baptist). Larger congregations should also be
able to cover the lesser known stories.

15

☐ *The Jesse tree*

When the groups are ready, ask them to choose a symbol to depict the event or person chosen.

For example:

ADAM

JOSEPH

NOAH

SOLOMON

Draw as many of these symbols as desired onto card, and cut them out.

Produce a Jesse tree, which has been created by putting a large branch of a tree into a flower-pot filled with earth.

When all the groups have finished making the symbols encourage everyone to come out and hang their symbol from the Jesse tree.

tional: | Use the freeze-frame drama technique to depict some of the Old
Drama | Testament stories. See 3rd Sunday in Lent for information
regarding this.

Watch some of these and invite the congregation to guess the
stories depicted. The remainder could be watched over coffee
afterwards, or used later in the service.

☐ *Conclusion*

Encourage everyone to try to identify all the symbols on the tree –
without asking the groups who made them for help.

Simply close this part of the service by commenting that all the
characters and stories shown on the Jesse tree prefigured Jesus.
Their work spoke of the coming of Jesus, for it was their
responsibility to prepare the people for the arrival of the Messiah.

3rd SUNDAY IN ADVENT

The forerunner

John the Baptist came from the wilderness to speak to the Jewish
people. He was a wild, demonic-looking man, yet some of his
words made sense. God also speaks today through unlikely
sources.

Matthew 11.2–15

A number of pictures of optical illusions.
An overhead projector or board and paper, and felt-tip pens.
A set of questions on an overhead transparency, or large
    sheet of paper.
Paper and pencils, if desired.
A teenager to act as John the Baptist, if desired.
Words for the litany.
Candles, if desired.

☐ *Introduction: Optical illusions*

Use any pictures that can be seen from different perspectives as a
basis for looking at well-known objects in different ways. Or

enlarge the examples below to use on an overhead projector or board so that the whole congregation can see them.

Spend time looking at the pictures, making sure as far as possible that everyone can see the two perspectives. How many can see each perspective? How long does it take to see both? Is it possible to switch between the two?

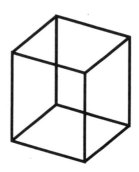

Optional
activity:
If I were ...

Alternatively, carry out the following exercise to help people look at things in a different way. Ask the congregation to use their imagination, to help them learn more about themselves and each other.

In pairs, invite them to ask the questions below first of themselves and then of a neighbour. Initially the work should be done in silence. When completed, share the results with one another. Adults will need to work with very young children. Conclusions could be written down.

- 'If I were a tree, I'd be a ...' (for example, an oak, ash, or poplar).

- 'If I were a piece of music, I would be ...' (a hymn, some brass band music, lullaby).

- 'If I were an item in the church, I would be ...'

After everyone has discussed this with someone else, see what they have learnt about themselves.

☐ *Comment*

Refer to the Gospel reading (Matthew 11.2–15), and comment that the people who came to hear John the Baptist needed to look at him in a different way. He looked like a wild man dressed in skins and living off the land, but he spoke like a prophet of old, telling them they must repent and be baptized. Yet they knew him – he was one of them, for his father was Zechariah the priest. How could he be a prophet?

Optional | Have a fairly unlikely person, perhaps a teenager, come forward to harangue the congregation in the style of John the Baptist. Use modern language and aim for realism so that the congregation are left saying, 'Who does he think he is speaking to us like that?' The speech could include any of the following comments:

'You're hypocrites, only paying lip service to Christianity! Repent!'

'If you continue to live as you do, then disaster will shortly occur! Repent!'

'There is only a short time left before the judgement day! Repent!'

The congregation might like to discuss their feelings of anger, irritation or amusement after the interruption. Ask how they might have felt about the real John the Baptist.

☐ *Discussion*

Finally, consider with the congregation the question of who are today's prophets. Where do warnings come from now? Is it possible to find them in unlikely places? Lastly, consider how God calls them now to repentance in this season of Advent.

 Concentrate today on prayers of repentance, praying for the sins of the whole world. Use different ages to represent different sins.
    Alternatively, use the litany from the Alternative Service Book.
    Light candles as a focal point for each separate prayer.

Note: If you are intending to create a display concerned with the memorabilia of baptismal material for the 1st Sunday after Christmas, you will need to initiate this project now.

4th SUNDAY IN ADVENT

The Annunciation
The Annunciation is looked at through a study of Old Testament expectations about the Messiah.

Zechariah 2.10–end

A potter with some clay or an artist and a painting, or a
   child with some lego bricks.
Bibles.
Copies of Bible quotations.
Hymn books.
Copies of pictures for children.
Sugar-paper, pencils or crayons, pens and paints.

☐ *Introduction: Demonstration*
Invite someone to join you who can either make pottery or paint.
Alternatively, ask a child who enjoys creating 'villages' or 'cars'
out of lego. Allow the person to bring as much equipment as
possible and demonstrate how they do their particular activity, or
invite them to discuss the subject with you.

☐ *Comment*
The Old Testament reading (Zechariah 2.10–end) reminds us that
God became human. This is the same as the potter (or artist or
child) becoming a part of their own creation, as though they
become a part of the item they have made.
    For God to become a human being was equally as amazing for
he didn't become a king with wealth and power, but a helpless
baby living in great poverty in a stable.

☐ *Groupwork: The Messiah*
Remind the congregation that the Jews had been waiting for the

Messiah – the one who was to save them – for centuries and that the Old Testament is full of references to him. To know Jesus better we must look at these expectations about the Messiah.

Create groups as indicated below, to look at some of these references. Alternatively use only one activity for the whole congregation.

GROUP A (ADULTS AND TEENAGERS)
Ask the group to examine the following Bible references for names of the Messiah. How many can they find?

Isaiah 9.6–7	Isaiah 8.14	Isaiah 11.1
Isaiah 53.3–12	Jeremiah 23.5	Jeremiah 23.6
Ezekiel 34.23	Psalm 110.4	Mark 14.62
Luke 9.44		

Make a poster of the names with their references for others to read, and put it up somewhere in church.

GROUP B (ADULTS AND TEENAGERS)
Ask the group to examine the following Bible references to find out what the Israelites expected of the Messiah. Give out the readings to different group members, and work in twos if desired.

Isaiah 7.14–16   Isaiah 9.4–5   Isaiah 9.6–7
Isaiah 11.1–5   Isaiah 11.10   Isaiah 40.10–11
Isaiah 42.1–4   Isaiah 53.3–12   Isaiah 61.1–2
Jeremiah 23.5–6   Ezekiel 34.23   Micah 5.1–5
Zechariah 9.9

Ask them to write up their conclusions on sugar-paper and put
up for all to read.

GROUP C (CHILDREN AND A COUPLE OF ADULTS)
Enlarge the pictures below for the children to colour. If desired
they could look up the Bible references. Encourage them to talk
about the Jews' expectations regarding the Messiah.

GROUP D (MIXED AGES OR ADULTS ONLY)
Ask the group to look at some traditional advent hymns. What kind of Messiah do they show?

Example:
Hark the glad sound
The Lord will come and not be slow
On Jordan's bank the Baptist's cry
O come, o come Immanuel
Come Thou long-expected Jesus

Encourage them to write up their conclusions on sugar-paper, and include pictures of the different kinds of Messiah shown.

☐ *Conclusion*
Hold a short plenary session to allow the groups to see each other's work, and close with a simple reminder that 'the Creator became a part of his own creation', or 'our God became human', in all these different ways: prophet, priest, king, and suffering servant.

CHRISTMAS DAY
(or Christingle Service)

God's light in our life
A stained-glass window or picture is used to speak about the light of Christ in our lives.

Isaiah 9.2 and 6–7   Hebrews 1.1–5   John 1.1–14

> A 'stained-glass window' made from tissue paper, or a small stained-glass picture.
> A light source from a window, candle, torch or overhead projector.
> A few adults and children with some prayers and candles.

☐ *Introduction: The stained-glass window*
In the previous week make a 'stained-glass' picture out of card and tissue paper (see instructions below) or find a small

stained-glass picture of the kind hung in windows. Stained-glass windows in church can be referred to, but you will also need a stained-glass picture.

How to make the 'stained-glass' picture

1. Find a simple picture, perhaps of a cross or a candle, and enlarge it. (Use a photocopier if possible as lines in the original picture will then create the 'leaded' effect.)
2. Pin the picture onto black sugar-paper, and cut round all the 'leaded' lines except those on the *outside*. Only the *inner* lines of the picture should be cut. Make sure that a border is left.
3. Fill in the picture with coloured tissue paper, changing the colour to suit the different parts of the picture. Use Pritt Stick to glue the tissue paper to the back of the picture.

□ *Discussion*

Hold the stained-glass picture up before the congregation and discuss how it was made. What does the picture show? Ask if other people have made these or possess small glass pictures to hang in the window.

Finally, admit that the picture, although attractive, is a little dull. Point out that it really needs a light source behind the 'glass'. Stained-glass windows in churches (possibly in yours) never look very good from outside, you need to go inside and see them when the light is bright outside.

Ask for suggestions as to how your picture might be improved. Then hold it up against a light source, for example, a candle, torch, or an OHP (overhead projector) light angled towards it. The picture will suddenly appear in all its glory, with the colours bright and attractive!

□ *Comment*

As you admire the stained-glass picture suggest that people are just like the picture. We might seem fairly attractive; we might seem to be happy, loving or kind people; but it is only when Christ's light shines through us that we appear really bright and fresh. Christ's light can be said to shine through us when we ask him into our lives.

Refer to the readings, which mention the 'light of God' (Isaiah 9.2, 6–7, Hebrews 1.1–5, and John 1.1–14). Isiaiah says that the child who is to be born will shine like a light in the darkness; the writer of Hebrews says the Son of God is the 'radiant light of God's glory'; and the Gospel reading picks up Isaiah's idea that the light of God will shine in the darkness, but the darkness will not overcome it.

May God come and shine in our lives, this day.

Optional This talk could be expanded to look at Jesus 'the light of the world' who was born at Christmas as a light in a dark world. Explore how even the feeble light of a candle makes the dark seem even darker. How much more does the light of Jesus make the dark (which we can think of as sin and evil) seem darker? The use of candles would be most effective.

You might wish to explore what 'inviting Jesus into our lives' might mean for the congregation. What would be the effect on our life this Christmas?

Alternatively, if your church possesses stained-glass windows, particularly those that are old, this talk could be expanded to include a look at medieval glass and modern glass. Notice the rich hue of the older glass. It may not be so vibrant in its colour, but its beauty is undeniable and it can make the new glass look garish. Compare this to older Christians in the community, not those older in age, but those who are spiritually mature. (This is from an idea by Sue Toogood.)

☐   *Conclusion*
Place the stained-glass picture somewhere it can be seen with a light source behind it for the rest of the service.

 Ask three or four adults or children to create simple prayers on different themes. As each comes forward, they should light a candle and place it on the altar or some other central point.

 Note: Sing 'Shine Jesus, shine' (WS) or 'The Spirit lives to set us free' (SGP).

1st SUNDAY AFTER CHRISTMAS

The Presentation
A crossword is used to talk about the theme of 'The Presentation'.
Just as both Eli and Jesus are presented to God, so one day we
shall be presented to God.

1 Samuel 1.20–end   Luke 2.22–40

Forewarn the congregation that they will be tested on the
readings.

An overhead projector or board.
Crosswords written on transparencies or large
    sheets of paper.
Two volunteers to write up the answers.
Copies of the Bible, if desired.
An Alternative Service Book, or Book of Common
    Prayer.
Memorabilia concerning baptisms.
Sugar-paper, Pritt Stick, Pritt-Tack, or map pins.

☐   *Introduction*
Inform the congregation that you are going to ask them to help to
solve a crossword based on the Old (or New) Testament reading,
without allowing them to look up the answers in their Bibles.
Comment that the church doors are *not* locked, but you hope they
will stay to explore the day's theme in greater depth!

☐   *Crossword*
Choose either crossword A or B to look at the theme of 'The
Presentation', and write the crossword on an overhead
transparency or large sheet of paper, omitting the answers! Ask
for two volunteers to write up the answers.
  You might decide to address the clues to different age groups or
types of people. For example, 'Will all those people with brown
hair answer this question?' Or, you might decide to create teams
to compete against each other.
  Suggest that hands are raised, as this will allow you to choose a
variety of different people to answer the questions. You may have
to be fairly tough over this!

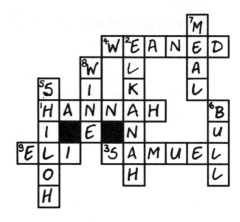

CROSSWORD A: ELI (1 SAMUEL 1.20–END)

Across

1 She had no children. (6 letters)
2 This baby was very wanted. (3 letters)
4 He couldn't go anywhere until he was _ _ _ _ _ _. (6 letters)
9 The boy was presented to this person: who was he?
(3 letters)

Down

2 The husband of the lady of 1 across. (7 letters)
5 They went here to make a sacrifice. (6 letters)
6 The woman took the animal to sacrifice to God. (4 letters)
7 This food was offered to God. (4 letters)
8 This drink was offered to God. (4 letters)

CROSSWORD B: JESUS (LUKE 2.22–40)

Across

1 Where is the Temple? (9 letters)
3 Offered to the Lord. (11 letters)
4 The law of this person had to be obeyed. (5 letters)
8 This person took Jesus in his arms and blessed God.
(6 letters)
10 Jesus will be a light to these people. (6 letters)

Down

2 Coming ritually clean. (8 letters)
5 Who was Jesus presented to at the temple? (4 letters)
6 These could be offered as a sacrifice. (11 letters)
7 Alternatively, these could be sacrificed. (7 letters)
9 A prophetess. (4 letters)
11 The prophetess's tribe. (5 letters)

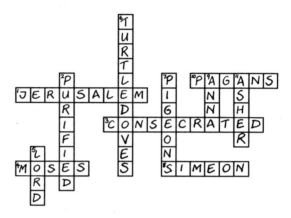

☐ *Comment*

Just as Eli (or Jesus), was *presented* to God, so we were *presented* to God at our baptism (or dedication) by our sponsors or Godparents.

If we were children they spoke for us, undertaking to see that we were brought up in the Christian faith. If we were adults then they were instrumental in supporting us in our new life.

One day we shall be presented to God again, this time at our death. Then we shall be presented by Jesus himself who will stand as our sponsor before God the Father.

Optional
- In the weeks beforehand invite the congregation to bring memorabilia from their own baptism. Then during the service create a display around the theme of 'Godparents', using photographs, training material, and the promises undertaken by Godparents. Encourage everyone to talk about their baptism (or someone else's) as the display is organized.
- Alternatively, discuss in small groups how your church might undertake to sponsor children and adults who are to be baptized. Begin the planning for a programme of nurturing new and young Christians.

2nd SUNDAY AFTER CHRISTMAS

The Light of the World
Today's service explores the theme of light and dark, and reminds us that Jesus is the Light of the World.

Isaiah 60.1–6   Matthew 2.1–12, 19–23

As many small candles as possible and some matches.
One large candle on a pedestal.
Overhead projector or board and paper, and felt-tip pens.
Crayons or coloured pencils, and paper as desired.
Materials for a collage and Pritt Stick, if desired.
A copy of *The Owl Who Was Afraid of the Dark* by Jill
     Tomlinson (Methuen 1992)
Collect for 2nd Sunday after Christmas.
Words for the litany.

☐ *Introduction*
Put out all the lights in the
church including any candles. Do
this deliberately and slowly,
and in silence. When it is dim,
light one large candle placed near
or in the middle of the congregation.
Again carry out this action slowly
and in silence. Allow everyone to
watch the flame for a moment
until you sense they are becoming
restless.

☐ *Buzz groups*
Do not put the lights on again, but ask everyone to turn to
another person and comment on their thoughts about the one
candle and its light.

☐ *Word association: 1*

At this point either break into small groups or encourage the congregation to work together as one group. Gather from them words associated with the candle and its light.

Finally, put all the lights on in the church and write up the words on an overhead projector or board. For example:

warmth	heat
fire	light
peace	flame
goodness	shine
Jesus	

Refer to the Old Testament reading (Isaiah 60.1–6) where God's glory is seen as light, and the Gospel reading (Matthew 2.1–12, 19–23) where we see the Wise Men following a star.

Remind the congregation that Jesus is called the 'light of the world', and that it was because of a light (a star) that the Gentile world first heard about the 'King of the Jews'.

☐ *Meditation*

Ask the congregation to hold the images of light which they have collected in the word association in their minds and apply them to Jesus. Allow a moment of silence. To help the younger children you may wish to suggest that Jesus makes us feel happy and warm rather like a flame, then ask them to think of other things that make them feel happy and warm.

The adults may find it difficult to compare some of the more violent images, for example, roaring flames. However remind them that God is not only a God of peace, and that all too often we attempt to tame God by the use of gentle images!

☐ *Comment*

Jesus, the 'light of the world', was born into a dark world. Look at the Gospel reading (Matthew 2.1–12, 19–23), and the example of Herod who wished to kill Jesus. Our world is not very different. Look at topical examples from the newspapers or television, as appropriate, but finally comment that just as a candle flame makes the darkness seem darker, so Jesus shows up the evil in our world.

Optional
groupwork

GROUP A: PAINTING

1. Paint 'dark and light' pictures of the world. One side of the page should represent good aspects of creation or of the world today, and be painted in light, bright colours. The other side of the paper will represent the evil side of the world, and should be painted in dark, sombre colours.

The dark side could show industry spewing out polluted waste; poisonous rivers; vandalism; or murder; while the light side could show the beauty of the natural world; human beings helping one another; hospitals; or joyous worshipping faces.

2. Alternatively, create a huge collage using scraps of material, to represent darkness and light.

GROUP B: HAIKUS

Create haikus on the subject of 'Light and Dark'.

A haiku is a Japanese form of poetry consisting of three lines, with five syllables in the first line, seven in the second, and five in the last line. Ideally words are brainstormed on the theme suggested, then the mind is freed to put down whatever thoughts come into the head. However, encourage members of the group not to panic about the form. They should simply *create*!

GROUP C: DISCUSSION

Discuss what effect light has on dark – both literally and figuratively – by imagining a candle set in the middle of a dark and empty room. What effect does it have on the dark? Then ask questions like: 'Does a good person attract evil?' and 'Why did Jesus attract so much criticism?'

GROUP D: STORY-TIME

Read *The Owl Who Was Afraid of the Dark* by Tomlinson, and if there is time discuss the story afterwards.

☐ *Conclusion*

Finally, light as many candles as possible and allow a moment of silence before leading the congregation in saying the Collect for the 2nd Sunday after Christmas (Alternative Service Book).

Create a litany for the intercessions. Use the refrain:

Leader: Jesus, light of the world. Lord of all light:
All: Keep us ever in your light.

Optional

Note: Give out small candles. Light them and sing 'The spirit lives to set us free, walk, walk in the light' (SGP). The candles should then be taken home so that they will symbolically 'spread the light'. (This is from an idea by Carol Marsh.)

EPIPHANY

Showing forth Jesus to the world
The congregation are encouraged to look at the Wise Men and see what they have to say to us today.

Matthew 2.1–12

> Three adults to act as Wise Men.
> Suitable costumes and gifts for the Wise Men.
> A manger and some straw.
> A 'baby' in swaddling clothes.
> A copy of T. S. Eliot's poem 'Journey of the Magi', if
>   desired.

☐ *Introduction*
Ask the congregation to sit down while the lights are dimmed. Leave one central light over the point where the Wise Men will create their tableaux. If possible black out windows to enhance the effect.

Place a manger and 'baby' under the central light, and ensure no one is seated beyond this point (for instance choir or organist) during the sermon slot. They can return to their normal seating later.

☐ *The tableaux*
Dress three men up as the Wise Men as follows:

Caspar A young fresh-faced man with no beard. He carries frankincense.

Melchior An old man with grey hair and a beard. He carries gold.

Balthasar Preferably someone of African or Asian appearance, who is middle aged. Alternatively someone of swarthy appearance with 'designer stubble'. He carries myrrh.

Note that the three men chosen to act the parts of the Wise Men only have to enter the church, walk down the aisle and stand *facing away* from the congregation. This should help with recruitment!

However, ensure that the men's clothes are the most luxurious you can find. Aim to suit the build and appearance of the individual concerned, so that it looks completely natural on them.

The Wise Men should enter from the back of the church as the lights are dimmed and walk slowly down the church towards the spotlight and the manger. Ensure that a large gap is left between the men to enhance the majesty of the occasion. As they reach the manger they individually acknowledge the child with regal bows (which should be in character) before taking up positions to one side, but in front of the manger. At this point they still retain their presents.

Ensure that the Wise Men turn their faces and bodies *partially or completely* away from the congregation. The congregation will now be able to observe the Wise Men without being distracted by the people who are playing these parts.

Try also to ensure that the Wise Men take up slightly different positions so that they are not in a straight row for instance. The final tableau should be artistically pleasing!

☐ *Comment and discussion*

Allow the people to observe the Wise Men in the tableau position for a moment before continuing. Keep the lights out, except for any focused on the tableau.

Start by asking the congregation about any nativity plays they might have gone to before Christmas. Were the Wise Men included? Question whether they put the Wise Men in their crib scenes before Christmas. In this case they may wonder why you are looking at the Wise Men now, when Christmas feels as though it is over.

However, remind them that **today** is the Feast of Epiphany when we remember the coming of the Wise Men to the infant Jesus. Add that you are therefore going to look at the Wise Men today in some detail.

Using the tableau as your visual aid continue by giving the congregation as many of the facts below as desired:

Are the Wise Men fact or fiction?

- Much of the information we have about the Wise Men is contained in myth. We might think of myth as a story that explains how something happened (e.g. like how the world was created).

- Early stories mentioned twelve Wise Men, though now tradition says there were only three.

- Later they were called 'Kings' and given names: Caspar, Melchior and Balthasar.

- Sometimes these men are called 'The Magi' – men who were skilled in philosophy and medicine, and who could

---

interpret dreams. In Persia they were men of great repute, though in later times some of their number were little more than soothsayers and charlatans.

● We are told they followed a star to find Jesus. Many different suggestions have been made about this. Was it Halley's comet which was certainly visible in the sky about 11BC? Whatever the star was, people certainly believed that unusual occurrences in the heavens often spoke of great events on earth, and at this time there is much written evidence that many people were expecting the coming of a king.

● And what about the gifts?

Gold for a king. It was the custom to approach kings with a gift, and what gift is more suitable. It reminds us that Jesus is a king.

> (Melchior turns and presents the baby Jesus with his gift of gold before resuming his place, as the words about gold are spoken.)

Frankincense for a priest. This was used in the Temple at times of worship, and it reminds us that Jesus is a priest, and that he mediates (acts as a 'go-between' or 'bridge') between humans and God.

> (Caspar repeats Melchior's action above.)

Myrrh for one who is to die. This costly item was an ingredient in the oil used for anointing the dead, and it reminds us that Jesus came into the world to live and to die for us.

> (Balthasar repeats Melchior's action above.)

● The word 'epiphany' means 'showing forth'. Perhaps the most important thing of all is that this is the first sign that Jesus was to be the saviour of all humankind, and not just of the Jewish people, for his birth is welcomed by three Wise Men who come from outside Israel.

> (The three Wise Men should now turn and kneel before the manger, and remain kneeling during the prayers which follow.)

□ *Conclusion*

Conclude by reading a part of T. S. Eliot's poem 'Journey of the Magi', or close with a short prayer.

(The Wise Men should then stand, bow towards the manger and return in the same stately way through the congregation and out the door.)

1st SUNDAY AFTER EPIPHANY

Revelation: the Baptism of Jesus

We are reminded that God chose to call us to be his people. Each one of us has been specially chosen and given new life, even though we have done nothing to deserve this great honour.

Ephesians 2.1–10

> A copy of words for the game and someone to call the instructions.
> A copy of the stilling exercise.
> A copy of the guided meditation.
> Reports of projects started in Advent if desired.

□ *Introduction*

Initiate a game that calls one or two people out from the congregation. The call will not be obvious to others. Describe the person concerned including information that only they would know.

Example:

'The person I am thinking of has short hair, a wide mouth, laughs a lot, has been to Cornwall, likes fish and chips, knows the name of my cat, stayed indoors last night, hates football, wrote two letters last Sunday, and lives in a house with a pink door in Bolton . . .'.

Keep the instructions fairly general for as long as possible, so that a number of people think it might be them.

Request people not to put their hands up or come out, until all the instructions are completed. If a mistake occurs there isn't much you can do without hurting the person concerned.

☐ Discussion

Discuss with the congregation what it was like to wait, not knowing if they were going to be called. Who will admit to believing they were the person, until near the end of the description? What did it feel like having to own up to the call and actually come out to the front of the congregation?

☐ Comment

The New Testament reading (Ephesians 2.1–10), continues this theme. The writer says that when we were 'dead through our sins he brought us to life with Christ'.

God chose us and called us not because of any action of ours, but simply out of his great goodness.

Refer to the Gospel reading (John 1.29–34). It is at his baptism that Jesus is revealed as God's Son, and as the one who will baptize with the Holy Spirit.

Our response to God is to answer the call, and to thank him for his love for us.

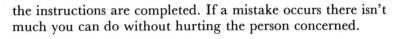

☐ Guided meditation

Allow the congregation to experience something of what God's call might be like by carrying out the following guided meditation. Make sure you stress it is all right to opt out and just sit with eyes closed.

Start with a stilling exercise like the following, and when everyone is suitably relaxed continue with the guided meditation.

STILLING EXERCISE
Close your eyes ... Notice your breathing ... in ... out ... Tense your toes ... flex your muscles and relax them ... Then your whole foot ... your leg ... bottom ... stomach ... body ... shoulders ... arms ... hands ... neck ... head ... face ... eyes ... nose ... mouth.

> **MEDITATION**
> *You are lying down ... so comfortable ... perhaps you're in bed ... or lying on the beach ... It's warm and cosy ... You're snuggled down ... half asleep ... Another moment you will be asleep ... You're just drifting off ...!*
>
> *Suddenly you hear a voice ... a voice you almost recognize ... It's calling someone ... Who's it calling? You can just make out the voice ... It's calling you ...*
>
> *You're almost too asleep to answer ... but you know that voice, surely ... Who is it ...?*
>
> *Go towards the voice ... happy that you've been called ... eager to reach him ...*

☐ *Conclusion*

Gently bring everyone back to the present, and remind the congregation that God *chose* each of us and *called* us. All that is left to us is to respond to his call – again and again!

Optional | If on the 1st Sunday in Advent you chose to initiate a variety of projects under the title 'Project Hope' to help 'the hungry, the thirsty, the stranger, the naked and the sick', you may wish to use much of the time this week to hear reports on these projects.

2nd SUNDAY AFTER EPIPHANY

Revelation: the first disciples
An in-depth survey of the disciples is carried out to look at what we really know about them.

John 1.35–end

A number of group leaders as desired.
Bibles.
Scrap paper and pencils.
Bible references.
Any reference books about the disciples or copies of the information below.

Copies of the emblems of the disciples.
Sugar-paper, glue, paints and pens as necessary.

□ *Introduction*

Inform the congregation that the theme for the day is 'The first disciples' and you are hoping that everyone will use the time available today to find out more about at least *one* of the disciples – whether this is about their life when Jesus was alive, or after his death. The information will then be used to produce a group display based on each disciple/saint concerned.

□ *Groupwork*

Create groups and allocate one or more disciples to each group. You may wish to give a group two disciples if the Bible references to them are few, or the group is large. Alternatively one or two people working on their own might be happier with one of the lesser-known disciples.

Give the groups concerned a copy of the appropriate Bible references, one or more Bibles, and a sheet of scrap paper and a pencil. Ask them to look up and read all the references. When the group feel they have discovered enough about their disciple ask them to produce a group offering based on him. Any of the following media would be suitable:

drama	painting or drawings
mime	written work about the saint
freeze-frame drama (see 3rd	emblems of the saints
Sunday in Lent for instructions)	prayers based on the disciples
banners	poetry
frieze work	stories.

formation
on the ST PETER
disciples

Legend has it that St Peter refused to be crucified in the same manner as Jesus, and chose to die on an inverted cross. The keys symbolize the keys to the kingdom of heaven.

References:
Luke 5.1–11; Mark 1.29–31; Matthew 10.2–5, 14.29; Mark 8.29;

Luke 9.28–36, 22.7–13, 22.31–4; Matthew 26.69–75; John 13.4–11, 13.21–5; John 20.1–10; Acts 1.15–26, 2.14–36, 4.1—5. end, 8.14–25, 10.1–end, 12.1–end, 15.7–11; Galatians 2.14.

ANDREW

According to tradition Andrew was crucified on an X shaped cross.

References:
Matthew 4.18–20; Mark 1.29, 13.3–4; John 1.35–42, 6.5–9, 12.20–23; Acts 1.12–13.

JAMES

The shells refer to James being on pilgrimage as he was the first disciple to have gone on a missionary journey.

References:
Mark 1.19–20 and Luke 5.10–11; Matthew 10.2, 17.1–8; Mark 14.32–42; Acts 12.1–3.

JOHN

The emblem refers to the legend that St John was offered a poisoned chalice with which to kill himself.

References:
Mark 1.19–20 and Luke 5.10–11; Matthew 20.20–23; Luke
9.49–50, 22.7–13; John 19.26–7, 13.23–6, 20.1–10 (all understood
to be John); Acts 1.12–14, 3—4, 8.14–17.

PHILIP

Jesus addressed his words concerning the feeding of the multitude
to Philip and the roundels represent two loaves of bread.

References:
John 1.43–46; Matthew 10.1–6; John 12.20–23; Acts 1.13–14;
John 14.8–11; Acts 8.4–13; 8.26–40 (check which Philip –
evangelist or apostle.

BARTHOLOMEW

Bartholomew was believed to have been flayed alive and
crucified.

References:
Matthew 10.2–6; Acts 1.12–14.

MATTHEW

The moneybags remind us that St Matthew was a tax collector,
known as Levi.

References:
Matthew 9.9; Mark 3.14–19; Acts 1.12–14.

THOMAS

Thomas is the patron saint of builders and is said to have built a church with his own hands in India. He was apparently speared to death.

References:
Matthew 10.2–4; John 11.11–16, 14.1–7, 20.24–9, 21.1–14; Acts 1.12–14.

JAMES THE SON
OF ALPHAEUS

The symbol refers to the tradition that James was thrown down from the top of the Temple in Jerusalem, stoned and sawn in two by the Jews.

References:
Matthew 10.2–4; Acts 1.12–14.

SIMON
THE ZEALOT

Simon was the companion to St Jude on many missionary journeys and was known as a great fisher of men through the power of the gospel.

References:
Matthew 10.2–4 and Luke 6.13–16.

JUDAS (ALSO KNOWN
AS JUDE, THADDEUS,
AND LEBBAEUS)

The ship represents the church which Judas took to many places on his journey as a missionary.

References:
Luke 6.13–16; John 14.22–4; Acts 1.12–14.

JUDAS ISCARIOT

Judas accepted thirty pieces of silver to betray Jesus. He committed suicide and was buried in a field he had bought for this purpose.

References:
Matthew 10.1–4; John 6.66–71; Mark 14.10, 14.43–50; Luke 22.3–6; 22.47–53; John 13.26–30; 18.2–11; Matthew 27.5; Acts 1.18.

☐ *Conclusion*
Put up as much wall-work as possible during the service, or arrange to create a full display during the following week ready for next Sunday.

If possible see any drama or mime, and use any prayers, during this service. Otherwise make sure that any offerings are picked up and used at a later date.

No comment should be necessary – all the connections and learning will have been going on during the work.

3rd SUNDAY AFTER EPIPHANY

Revelation: signs of glory
God's love for us is often revealed in signs and symbols.
Recognizing these symbols is important for a Christian.

John 6.1–14

Ordnance Survey map symbols produced on an overhead
  projector or board, and a felt-tip pen.
Bibles.
Group leaders, if desired, and copies of instructions.
Additional crosses hidden for Group B, if desired.
Picture of a dove for Group C.
Sugar-paper and pens.

☐ *Introduction*

Introduce a number of symbols that are used on Ordnance
Survey maps to the congregation by putting these up on an
overhead projector or board. Use some that will be recognized by
children, and some that even the adults will find difficult.

The symbols could include:

Footpath	------- FOOTPATH
Church	✝ CHURCH
Youth Hostel	▲ YOUTH HOSTEL
Parking	**P** PARKING
Footbridge.	FOOTBRIDGE

Ask the congregation to try to guess what they stand for, and use
the word 'symbol' as much as is practicable.

When all the symbols have been guessed, ask for a definition of
the word 'symbol'. One definition might be that a symbol is
something which represents something else. There may well be
other definitions, and the congregation may wish to choose one of
these.

☐ *Comment*

Point out that symbols are used extensively in the Christian faith.

They are often used as a quick way of saying something, and sometimes they are used as the only way of saying it. Sometimes we find it difficult to put everything into words and using a symbol is easier. For instance, in today's world we can hardly put long instructions on every road sign. A symbol is much easier. It is just the same with Christianity.

Today the congregation are going to look at some religious symbols.

☐ *Groupwork*

Create groups as follows:

GROUP A (ADULTS AND OLDER CHILDREN)
Read John 6.1–14 again. Bread and fish are both well-known Christian symbols. What do they mean in this passage? In other words, is this only a miracle, or are there other meanings?

The fish is also used as a symbol for Jesus Christ because the Greek word for fish uses all the first letters of the words 'Jesus Christ, Son of God, Saviour'.

Do members of the group know of any other symbols that are used for Jesus Christ? (Answers might include: shepherd, light, etc.)

GROUP B (ADULTS AND CHILDREN)
The cross is a symbol. What does it mean to different members of the group?

Notice that there are different kinds of crosses:

Go on a search throughout the church to see how many different kinds of crosses can be found. Ensure that group members look at windows and books, as well as up on the ceiling or floor!

(*Note:* You may wish to hide a few more interesting crosses around the church.)

GROUP C (ADULTS AND CHILDREN)
Produce a picture of a dove. The dove is a symbol of the Holy Spirit and also of peace.

Remembering all the violence and lack of peace in the world ask the group to create another symbol of peace to fit either their own locality, or the twenty-first Century.

Use sheets of sugar-paper and felt-tip pens to plan and draw this new symbol. Encourage the group to work together on one symbol.

A comment or prayer based on the group's discussion could be placed under the finished article if desired.

Optional groups If further groups are required create one group to look at symbols in the Eucharist, and another to look at symbols in the baptism or wedding services. Such groups might be more appropriate for adults.

☐ *Conclusion: Plenary session*
When the groups have concluded their work, come back together to share some of the results.

 If Group C created a prayer, use as appropriate.

4th SUNDAY AFTER EPIPHANY

Revelation: The new Temple

Just as the Samaritan woman begins to realize that God is not limited to places, we are encouraged to see that God is Spirit, and as such he is to be worshipped at all times and in all places.

John 4.19–26

> Overhead projector or board and paper, and felt-tip pen.
> Two 'scribes'.
> A slide show of pictures and music, if desired.

☐ *Introduction*

Look at the Gospel reading (John 4.19–26). Comment that the Samaritan woman is worried over Jesus' words. Note that all her life she has been brought up to believe that Mount Gerizim is the most sacred of places and that her worship should be addressed there.

Yet Jesus is not a Samaritan, he looks towards Jerusalem. Where, she must be thinking, should I go?

We must presume that she is taking a sin-offering to this holiest of places, for Jesus has just confronted her with her sin of having had five husbands as well as the man with whom she is now living.

But Jesus confounds her by dismissing Jerusalem *and* Gerizim. They are not important, he says. God is Spirit. He is not limited to places and to objects, and our gifts to him must therefore be gifts of the spirit.

☐ *Brainstorm*

Set up an overhead projector or board and paper. Appoint two scribes and invite the congregation to brainstorm the word 'church' to help them see that God is not limited to the church congregation on a Sunday morning, or indeed the church building!

Write the word 'church' in large letters at the top or in the middle of your sheet, and invite adults and children to shout any words that come into their heads connected with the word 'church'.

Make no comment on their choice of words, simply allow the scribes to add them to the list.

For example:

Church

singing	dark	choir
quiet	people	priest
worship	oppressive	happy
communion	psalms	

When the congregation have finished, carry out the same procedure with the word 'worship'.

□ *Discussion*

Finally, compare the two lists, rejecting at this stage if necessary any 'oddball' words that don't fit the overall pattern. Make sure, though, such decisions are collective.

Discuss the two lists. Are they similar? Are there differences? What kind of conclusions can the congregation come to about the two lists?

Note:

1. If the lists are almost the same it would seem that the congregation see worship as either only taking place when the congregation are assembled in church, *or* they are so liberated, that 'church' is synonymous with 'spirit'. You will need to interpret this!

If you feel the former is the case, try brainstorming the word 'spirit'. You will get 'ghost' and 'spook' but as you have been speaking about God as Spirit you should also get words that show that worship is seen as being wider than that which is happening in a building on Sunday.

2. If the lists are entirely different you may wish to reflect the realization that worship does not seem to be contained by forms and buildings.

Optional | Set up a working party to look further at what emerges and to report back to the PCC or church management group.

□ *Conclusion*

Hold a plenary session to draw together some of the observations and comments that have come up in the brainstorm sessions. You may wish to draw items from both sheets to create a third sheet that encompasses the core of both the others. This will contain those things held in common between 'church' and 'worship'. Decide with the congregation what this may teach you about yourselves.

Create a slide show of pictures in the week before the service, accompanied by music but with *no speech,* to allow individuals to say their own private prayers. Use headings written on card to accompany the pictures. For example:

Heading	Picture
The world:	pictures of violent action, war zones, famine or poverty.
The Church:	people of different religions or faiths.
The sick:	someone ill in hospital, or a picture of an elderly person.
The family:	parents and children enjoying some activity together.

5th SUNDAY AFTER EPIPHANY

Revelation: The wisdom of God
Human beings learn by using their senses. Sometimes we need to sharpen the focus of our senses in order to learn more about God.

1 Corinthians 3.18–end

> Items for as many of the activities suggested below as desired.
> A group of helpers will be needed to organize this sermon slot. The essence will be careful planning and the setting up of all the activities before the congregation enter the building.

☐ *Introduction*

The philosopher Berkeley once said that if we couldn't see, hear, touch, taste or smell something we had no proof that it existed.

He argued that when we left a room, unless we could see, hear, touch, taste or smell the objects in the room we had left, then we couldn't prove that they existed while we were outside the room.

His argument is logical, but nevertheless since the table and chair were in the room when we left and are there when we return our commonsense says they must obviously be there in our absence.

Our senses are also very important to us spiritually – far more important than we realize. We can be fired with love, repentance, or inspiration through another's speech; an autumn afternoon in woods or on the hills can fill us with joy or peace; the velvet ear of our favourite dog can fill us with thankfulness and love. All of these may speak to us of God. It is often through our senses that we learn about God.

☐ *Exploring the senses*

Encourage everyone (including the choir, organist and servers) to get up from their seats and go exploring. They can decide to try one of the activities, or one of the senses, or as many as they wish.

SIGHT

● Create a corner of the church concerned with light. Place a number of candles in the corner (using different shapes, colours and sizes) and light them. Place a mirror behind them, or put crystal objects nearby to reflect and catch the light. Alternatively, allow the light to fall on an object of great beauty or onto one that creates interesting shadows.

● Hang a mobile created from shiny foil, to catch the light.
● Put out cardboard, scissors and small pieces of cellophane, together with a template, to allow anyone to make coloured 'glasses'.
● Obtain a microscope and slides for people to use.
● Put out binoculars, a telescope, or a child's kaleidoscope.

- Obtain a sheet of braille writing, together with the alphabet and allow people to try to decipher this with their eyes closed.
- Place a bright light before a white wall or sheet and encourage people to make shadow puppets with their hands.

SOUND
- Create a tape of different noises and encourage people to guess the noises. You might wish to supply headphones for this activity.
- Supply a variety of musical instruments and ask people to see what noise they can make with them.
- Place some chairs in a corner and ask people to sit down, close their eyes, and listen to the noises in the church. These could be listed.
- Place some paper on a table and encourage the people to write down as many onomatopoeic words as they can (that is, words that sound like the action they refer to for example: buzzing, slap, pitter-patter).
- Provide the necessary materials for making a yoghurt-pot telephone: yoghurt pots, string, scissors, and an example of the finished product.
- Invite a deaf person to teach some signing words.
- Ask the choir to sing a special anthem or play some music.

TOUCH
- Create some 'feely' bags (material bags, with elastic in the top, filled with small interesting articles: a shell, some velvet, polystyrene, a large marble, etc.) and ask members of the congregation to guess the objects inside through 'touch' alone.
- Using someone as a model, ask people to close their eyes and touch the face and hair of the model. What does it feel like? Guess the person concerned. Encourage friends and relatives to feel each other's faces.
- Put out a table with paper and pencils and encourage people to draw round their hands. These could be used to create a collage or picture.
- Put out some ink pads and paper and ask people to make finger-print marks.
- Create poetry on 'My mother's (or father's) hands'.
- Invite a dancer to give a dance workshop on the theme of 'hands'.

TASTE
- Place a number of food items in different pots with lids on. Blindfold volunteers and ask them to taste each one before

guessing the contents. The following foods would be suitable: marmite, jam, salt, sugar and jelly.

- Have a variety of foods from different countries to sample, or food from one particular country.
- Have available a variety of fruits or vegetables from other countries for the congregation to try, e.g. guavas, lava bread, mangoes, zuchini.
- Ask people to close their eyes and picture their favourite food. Then ask them to imagine it with no taste. Or invite someone who has lost their taste to talk about the experience.

SMELL
- Burn some incense, joss-sticks, or a perfumed candle.
- Place a number of different perfumes on a small table and ask people to smell them. What happens when people smell a number of these?
- Cut up some apples and ask people to pick up a piece and smell it. Does the outside of the apple smell the same as the inside?
- Smell some lemons or oranges.
- Talk about people's favourite or most disliked smells.

☐ *Plenary session*
Finally gather the congregation back together and talk *briefly* with them about their experiences of this activity.

☐ *Conclusion*
It is important that we practice using our senses in order to learn more about God and about each other. How will God communicate through them if we have forgotten how to use our senses?

Add that there is another sense, however, one we might call the 'sixth sense'. Just as we believe that the table and chair are still in the room next door when we are absent, so we also believe other things we cannot prove. Sometimes we may feel that something is wrong with another person even when they are nowhere near us.

We might say that a 'sixth sense' seems to tell us this. All we know is that we cannot always prove everything through our five senses, or indeed through our intellect.

The New Testament lesson (1 Corinthians 3.18–end) reminds us that sometimes we have to ignore our senses and our intelligence. It is no good for instance using only our five senses or our intellect to prove the truth of Christianity.

We just have to rely on our sixth sense. For it is when we are not trying to be wise and clever that God speaks to us in different ways.

Burn incense while the prayers are said, and use a visual focus for 'eyes open' prayers.

Alternatively use slides or photographs to accompany the intercessions. Or play some music to accompany silent prayer.

 Note: 1. It would be highly appropriate to have a processional hymn in this service, or a hymn accompanied by actions. If the latter, ensure the actions are not too childish, and that they are known by everyone. A new action song that everyone has to learn might be appropriate. If you are not accustomed to processions or action songs – try them!

2. If you intend using the service for the 8th Sunday before Easter you will need to think about inviting a guest speaker now.

6th SUNDAY AFTER EPIPHANY

 Revelation: parables
God's revelation is made known to us through parables if only we will listen.

2 Samuel 12.1–10   Matthew 13.24–30

> Group leaders.
> Bibles and study guides as desired.
> Sugar-paper and coloured pencils or crayons.
> Sufficient 50p (or £1) coins for the whole congregation, and
>   forms to note the names of those receiving the coins.

☐ *Introduction*
Explain that a parable is an imaginary story based on an everyday and ordinary experience which teaches us a religious truth.

We tend to think that only Jesus told people parables, but this is not so. There are parables in the Old Testament (as in the reading set for today) and there are modern stories that are parables (e.g. the story of 'The Fuzzies' in *Flowers, Fonts and Fuzzies* by Carole Copland (Church House Publishing, 1986).

The one thing all parables have in common is that through them we learn more about God or the way in which he wants us to live.

☐ *Groupwork*

Set up a number of groups as desired and encourage the congregation to join one of the groups to learn more about parables.

GROUP A (ADULTS)
Study one of the other parables found in St Matthew's Gospel. For example:

The hard-hearted servant (18.23–35).
The workers in the vineyard (20.1–16).
The ten bridesmaids (25.1–13).

Use a study guide if desired. What does the parable have to say to us today?

GROUP B (CHILDREN)
With the help of an adult look at the parable of the hidden treasure (Matthew 6.19–21).
Enable the children to see that aiming to have the best bicycle, or trainers, is not what God wants. (These will get old and become out of date!) God wants us to put all efforts into perfecting ourselves and getting to know him.
Encourage the children to draw a banner *together* (in harmony) based on the parable.

GROUP C (ADULTS AND CHILDREN)
Study the parable of the Three Servants, or 'Talents' (Matthew 25.14–30) until the group begins to understand the parable.

Then produce some drama that depicts this parable, perhaps using modern examples: the Building Society, the Bank, the mattress.

Alternatively translate the money into gifts that God gives us for our use.

☐ *Project work: Using our talent for God*
Gather the congregation back together again when the group work is finished and inform them that you are initiating a project that will cause them to use the talents they possess that were given by God. It will also help to further God's work, because the money made will be going to charity. Name a specific charity or missionary work. You might wish to suggest the money goes to SPCK (The Society for Promoting Christian Knowledge) to help in their work of Christian education throughout the world.

Give each adult and child in the congregation 50p (or a £1) and ask them to go away and attempt to increase its value. Try to include, even small children, since they could work with sisters and brothers – to make marzipan sweets, for instance.

Offer some suggestions for those who might feel daunted:

- make biscuits or sweets (coloured marzipan) to sell;
- create new birthday cards out of old ones and sell them;
- knit a toy to sell;
- create birthday tags for presents out of old cards and sell them;
- buy a small sachet of car shampoo and clean someone's car at an economical rate.

Encourage the whole congregation to take part in the project. Ideally they should not simply add some money to that given, but should work to create the increase.

The more prudent will see the sense in working together, and in creating something very small initially, which will give them the capital to fund a larger project. They will also see the sense in keeping the cost of the item made, or service given, at a very low rate so that friends and family do get very good value for money and are not just forced to pay out of goodwill.

Keep a note of everyone who receives the money, and invite them back to a service in the future when the money can be handed in to be used for the charity you have chosen. You might wish to invite someone from the organization concerned to join you at this service.

☐ *Conclusion*
Make sure that the banner produced by Group B is used, perhaps as an altar frontal if some means of fixing it can be found. Also

include the drama produced by Group C at some point later in the service.

Conclude with a prayer of blessing on the projects about to be undertaken.

Note: If you feel that the church cannot afford to give 50p to each person make it clear that you will be reclaiming the 50p coins and deducting them from the money raised for charity.

9th SUNDAY BEFORE EASTER

Christ the teacher

Jesus was the greatest teacher we know – he taught people using the common experiences of life. We are reminded that we learn best from experience.

Luke 8.4b–15

> Overhead projector or board and paper, and felt-tip pen.
> Bibles as desired.
> Paper and pencils for groups.
> Coloured pencils or crayons and paper if desired.

☐ *Introduction*

Discuss with the congregation the best ways to learn anything, by asking the following questions:

- How does a baby learn that stairs are dangerous?
- How do we learn a fire is hot?
- How do we learn about car maintenance?
- How do we learn about the love of God? (You will need to deal with this answer if it is radically different to that given for the preceding ones.)

Put the conclusions up on a board for all to see. These will probably include some of the following observations:

- It helps to *see* for ourselves.
- It helps to *hear* someone else/read someone else's experiences.
- It helps to *experience* or *discover* something for ourselves.

Alternatively, encourage small groups to explore these questions in
discussion and report back after a few minutes to the whole
congregation.

☐ *Comment*

Refer to the fact that you can *tell* an adult or child not to touch
the fire, you can *show* them that the fire is hot, and they can also
experience the heat for themselves.

Note that they will learn that the fire is dangerous by any of
these means, but experience is usually the most effective.

Very often it is only when we experience things for ourselves
that we really learn.

'Jesus the teacher' is the theme of today's readings. Jesus knew
all about teaching. He stood in the fields around the Sea of
Galilee and he used the examples known to all his listeners (the
sower sowing seed, the woman using yeast to make bread, and the
fisherman trawling with his nets) to talk about God.

Add that if Jesus were here in the flesh today, he would
probably teach us using the things of our world: cars, aeroplanes,
and supermarkets.

☐ *Groupwork: A modern parable*

Encourage the congregation to divide up into mixed groups of
adults and children. Their task is to create a modern story based
on the parable of the sower. The modern parable can be told as a
story alone, or with mime, or with accompanying pictures by the
group.

If the congregation need further help you could suggest the following story-line:

'There were once four teenagers who heard about God.
Darren went to hear a famous evangelist at the local football stadium . . .
Sam picked up a Bible one night and began to read . . .
Tom went to his local church one Easter where to his surprise . . .
Paul heard about God through a friend who stopped to help him one night when . . .'

☐ *Conclusion*

It will probably be impossible to hear all the stories from the different groups, and some may not be completely finished. However, encourage the groups to perfect their efforts after the service and appoint someone to type the stories up into book form. These could then be sold or given to the congregation.

If any groups accompanied their story with mime use them in this or future services as appropriate.

Finally, remind the congregation that we need to help one another learn – not through words, but through our actions. Comment that every single person, whatever their age, is responsible for enabling other people to grow as Christians, in any way that they can.

Create a 'collage' of prayer by centring the intercessions around education:

- local schools, colleges
- governors
- parents
- education within the church (children/adults)
- pupils
- playgroups.

8th SUNDAY BEFORE EASTER

Christ the healer

All healing in this world is in some way part of God's work of healing and reconciliation, and we are reminded of this by looking at the work of hospitals and other health organizations.

2 Kings 5.1–14

Use the Dramatized Bible for this reading or accompany the reading with mime.

> One or more speakers.
> Displays of healing work, as desired.
> Overhead projector, or board and paper and felt-tip pen, as desired.
> Candles.

☐ *Introduction*

Comment that no matter who we are, or how influential our position in life we are all subject to illness. In the Old Testament reading (2 Kings 5.1–14) we see that Naaman, who is commander of the king's army and a very powerful man in the land, has caught leprosy.

Remind the congregation of the horror of this illness. The term 'leprosy' included a number of skin diseases, but the end results were the same – banishment from the tribe. For such a man as Naaman to catch this would have been horrific. Comment that Naaman had to learn to trust both Elijah and God.

We too sometimes have to learn this lesson when we or someone we love becomes ill. God will heal us but sometimes not in the way that we desire. God may see that we need spiritual healing far more than we need physical healing, or that we need to be forgiven. When we say that God always answers prayer we don't always mean that he says 'Yes' to what *we* want. His answer may be to say 'No!' to what we want. However we must note that God is still answering our prayer!

God also works through different people and in different kinds of ways. Sometimes it is only when we look back that we can see that God was present. Naaman too must have wondered where God was when he caught leprosy!

□ *Activities*
Continue following up the theme of healing in any of these ways:

GUEST SPEAKER
● Invite one or more speakers to give a brief talk about healing. If more than one speaker is used, try to ask people from totally different organizations: e.g. the local doctor, and someone working in the field of homeopathy.
  Suggested speakers could include representatives from:

  Sue Ryder Home
  Local baby care unit
  Leprosy mission
  A local hospice or other terminal-care unit
  Headway
  A local dentist.

● You may also wish to widen the subject to include other forms of healing, in which case the following organizations might be of help:

  Relate
  Samaritans
  Home Start
  Probation service.

● Encourage the speakers to bring visual aids and to speak to both children *and* adults. Give them a time limit.

DISPLAYS
● Encourage any of the above organizations to loan you display material and mount a display about 'health and healing' throughout your church. Or ask the local doctor's surgery to produce a display to include the work of people like the health visitor, and the midwife, as well as that of the baby, diabetic, or well-woman clinic.
● Encourage the congregation to look at the displays at this

point in the service, and ask questions of any of the professionals who may have come to the service.
- Leave the displays up for a least a week.

PRAYER FOR HEALING
- Invite someone to come to talk about the laying on of hands and healing services. Plan how this might occur over a period of time in your church.

- Create an up-to-date prayer list of those who need healing. Children can be encouraged to draw people or situations that need their prayers. Stress the need for some confidentiality. Allow some time for prayer.
- In the weeks to come begin to carry out the plans, and ensure that the prayer-list is adopted by the church.

WHAT IS HEALING?
- Initiate a brainstorm on 'What is healing?' Put up all the ideas as they come from the congregation onto an overhead projector or board and paper without comment. Then create groups to look at these. Can a simple answer be formed – for example, 'Health is wholeness', or 'Health is peace of mind'?
- If a guest speaker is involved, or if one group has helped to mount the display, consider whether you wish to offer the collection to this organization.

☐ *Conclusion*

Underline the thinking of the Old Testament lesson that we have to put our trust in those who heal, *and* in God. Comment that God may not answer our prayers in the way we want, but he will answer them and he will heal us in the way that he thinks we need healing.

Centre the prayers of intercession around healing in its widest sense.

Light a candle as each healing prayer is said. Or pray for people individually and light a candle for each person.

7th SUNDAY BEFORE EASTER

Christ the friend of sinners
In church we are often exhorted to confess our sins that we may
be forgiven. What exactly does this mean?

Colossians 1.18–23   John 8.2–11

Group leaders for each group.

Group A: A jug of water; sugar-paper, pens, paints or
magazines and Pritt Stick; paper for prayers, and ASBs.

Group B: Bibles; sugar-paper, magazines and Pritt Stick;
paper and pencils.

Group C: A story-teller and notes of the Bible story; paper
and pencils.

Group D: Cardboard, paper, pens, and Pritt Stick.

Note: The prayers of confession should be said after the sermon
slot.

☐   *Introduction*
Introduce the subject of 'being forgiven'. Each week in church we
are exhorted to confess our sins and be forgiven. What does this
mean? As the theme for the day is 'Christ the friend of sinners',
suggest that this gives you a chance to look again at what Jesus
does for us each week.

Refer to the New Testament reading (Colossians 1.18–23).
Because of our sins we are separated from God who is perfect
(and therefore sinless), but Jesus has made a bridge between us by
dying for us.

In the Gospel reading (John 8.2–11) we see Jesus saving a
woman from being stoned. He asks the crowd a simple question:
'Who is faultless among you – he shall throw the first stone.' No
human being has ever been perfect except Jesus, and so the crowd
disappear.

Often we use images of water to explain what is happening
when people are forgiven. We may say they are 'cleansed' of their
sins. It is as though the sin were washed away. The collect for the
day uses this idea.

☐ *Groupwork*

Create as many groups as desired.

GROUP A: WATER (ADULTS AND CHILDREN — A FAIRLY LARGE GROUP)

1. Discuss why we need water. Think of as many good reasons as you can for the importance of water. You might want to put them up on a sheet of paper.

Examples might be:
- keeping clean
- drinking
- baptism
- refreshing ourselves
- swimming
- cooking
- industry
- for plant growth.

2. Then divide the group up to complete the next two tasks:

a. Create a series of pictures to illustrate all the uses of water. These could be painted or drawn, or pictures cut from magazines. Talk about the way we use water as a symbol in church, for instance, to clean, refresh and wash.

b. Create prayers of confession and absolution: At our baptism we were 'cleansed' or 'washed' from our sins, and we 'died in the waters of baptism' to be raised to 'new birth' with Jesus.

Use these water ideas to write suitable prayers for adults and children, and answer the questions of any children or adults who may not be baptized. You might need to look up the actual words of the baptism service.

If possible allocate one person from this group to read the prayer of confession and/or absolution later in the service, while the other group hold up the pictures they have made to accompany the prayers. Offer a jug of water at the same time as a visual reminder of our baptism, and place on the altar.

GROUP B: RECONCILIATION (ADULTS)

1. The New Testament reading (1 Colossians 1.18–23) speaks of being reconciled to God through Jesus Christ.

Discuss the passage, looking at some of the following questions:
- What does the word 'reconciliation' mean to you?
- Why are we estranged or separated from God?
- Is it always necessary to pay a price, or to suffer to achieve

reconciliation? (Apply this to today's world if desired, perhaps with regard to the Middle East or Northern Ireland.)

- What do you consider our part to be in God's great plan of reconciliation?

2. Divide the group to complete the following tasks.

a. Create a collage out of magazine pictures to represent 'reconciliation'. You may wish to show world issues like famine or war, or local issues like the homeless or the poor to illustrate your theme of our estrangement from God. Alternatively, you may wish to show something more symbolic.

b. Create prayers of intercession that pick up the theme of reconciliation being between human beings and God. Try to link with the collage being prepared by the group so that people can remain with eyes open, but focused on the collage, during the prayers.

3. Allocate one or two people from your group to read the prayers of intercession later in the service, and arrange for the collage to be held as a focal point at this time.

GROUP C: BEING FORGIVEN (ADULTS AND CHILDREN)
1. The group leader or someone already prepared, should tell the story of the woman caught committing adultery through the eyes of one of the bystanders or a disciple (or even the woman herself). There is no need to go into great details regarding the meaning of 'adultery', particularly if there are younger children present, simply say 'she was in love with another man, who was not her husband'.

Note: If the story-teller has never tried this technique the following ideas might help. Mention:

- the strong feelings of the man and woman for each other, despite themselves.
- being caught, possibly kissing.
- the horror of knowing she would be stoned to death.
- being dragged in front of all those people.
- not daring to look up, but hearing Jesus' words.
- suddenly realising that she was free to go.
- the final promise made to herself not to do this again.

The story-teller should then write down the bare bones of the story, and tell it simply in his/her own words, not forgetting to look at the listeners.

2. Discuss how the woman must have felt. Have any of the group ever felt as the woman must have done when she was caught? What is it like to feel that the whole world has collapsed on top of you? Can the group remember what it feels like to be forgiven, particularly when they have done something dreadful?

3. If you are not going to use the ideas for Ash Wednesday this year ask the group to spend some time thinking about the things they have 'done wrong' recently. The group might like first to make a list of all the ordinary sins they have committed.
   For example:

   - lies
   - being big-headed
   - pride
   - desiring other people's possessions
   - hitting someone
   - thinking nasty thoughts
   - gossiping
   - being rude
   - being unkind.

Then encourage the group to close with a moment's silence, so that they can 'hold these and other sins before God in their hearts'. Close with the words 'Jesus said: You may go; do not sin again.'

GROUP D: THE CROSS OF FORGIVENESS (ADULTS AND CHILDREN)

1. Discuss the whole subject of 'sins', and create a list of as many possible sins as the group can think of, including those that are appropriate to children as well as to adults.

2. Then take a large piece of sugar-paper and draw or paint a large cross in the centre. Surround the cross with words of all shapes and sizes depicting the sins that the group has listed. Decide who will take this up to the altar later in the service.

3. Close this session by a few moments of silent, but 'open-eyed' prayer, encouraging everyone to concentrate on their own personal faults, and asking God to forgive them and help them to start afresh. End with the words 'Remove my sin, and I will be clean; Create a pure heart in me, O God' (Psalm 51).

Optional group | Young children may prefer to listen to the story of *Miles and the Computer* by Taffy Davies (Scripture Union 1987).

☐ *Conclusion*

Gather everyone back together. Use the prayers of confession and absolution, and the intercessions, as appropriate in the service. Place the cross collage and the water jug on the altar. Listen to the experiences of the different groups as desired.

You might wish to close this section by a moment's silence, for reflection.

ASH WEDNESDAY

 Preparing for Easter

Ash Wednesday is a time for being honest with ourselves and with God. Seeing ourselves as we really are can be an important part of our preparation for Easter.

Joel 2.12–17   Luke 18.9–14

> Large cross (preferably wooden) and some large nails.
> Paper, pencils, pens and labels.
> Container to burn papers in and matches.
> Large nails – one for each member of the congregation.
> A copy of *Lent, Holy Week and Easter* (CHP/CUP/SPCK 1986).

Note: Give each member of the congregation a sticky label and pen as they enter church, and encourage them to write their Christian name on the label and attach to their clothing.

☐ *Introduction*

Place a large, plain wooden cross in front of the congregation where it can be seen by everyone, along with some large nails.

Comment that Ash Wednesday starts the penitential period of preparation that leads up to the great celebration of Easter. Ash Wednesday is the first day of Lent – that time of inward searching as we begin to make ourselves ready for Easter.

Although Jesus died nearly two thousand years ago we are still responsible in our own way for the fact that he died. It can be said that each of our sins crucifies him again. (Pick up a large nail as you say this, and hold it before the congregation.)

☐ *Meditation: Negative thoughts*

Initially spend a moment or two looking at the words 'negative' and 'positive' so that even the youngest children will begin to understand what they mean when applied to their own actions.

Examples for younger children of negative actions might include:

 – the times they have hurt brothers or sisters;
 – lost their temper;
 – been rude.

Then hold at least five minutes' silent meditation, asking those present to think of all the negative things in their own lives. The cross and nails will act as a focal point for those who prefer not to close their eyes. Do not be put off by children who may fidget or be noisy – they could be encouraged to draw some negative things (e.g. hitting their brother, or wanting *all* the cakes).

Optional It might be helpful to ask everyone to think about their actions over a period of a few days, or that particular day, starting from the moment they opened their eyes.

The activities of the day before could be put up on a board (e.g. before breakfast, morning, lunch, afternoon, etc.) to help younger members, or those not accustomed to doing a meditation, to focus their minds on what has happened at each point in the day.

After about five minutes give out pencils and paper, and ask everyone to write down all their negative thoughts and actions. Younger children may need to work with adults.

When the task is completed, the pieces of paper should be

folded over once. Gather all the papers in and burn them in a suitable container and in a suitable place.

Ideally this should happen in church but having regard to your own circumstances and the fire risk, you might wish the congregation to follow you outside.

□ *Conclusion*

At the end ask each person to come out to the front of the church to receive the absolution. This should be done personally, using the information on the labels:

'Mark, may Almighty God have mercy upon you.'

You may also wish to sign each person's forehead with a cross. Ash could be used if desired (either by burning last year's palm crosses, or using the burnt confessions, as appropriate).

Finally, give each person a large nail. When everyone has returned to their seats mention that the nail should be kept somewhere where they will come across it often (in a pocket or handbag) to help them remember that each of their sins crucifies Jesus again. You may need to add a cautionary note for younger children, as well as smaller nails!

(This is from an idea by Chris Wagstaff.)

Use the litany of penance from *Lent, Holy Week, Easter* (CHP/CUP/SPCK 1986).

Note: Further liturgies for the beginning of Lent can also be found in *Lent, Holy Week, Easter*.

1st SUNDAY IN LENT

The King and the Kingdom: temptation
The penitential season of Lent begins with an acknowledgement of the things that tempt us to sin.

Hebrews 4.12 – end   Luke 4.1–13

An overhead projector or board and paper, and a felt-tip pen.

A 'top ten' list of temptations.
30 pairs of cards for young children, if desired.
Group leaders.
Copies of Psalm 139, if desired.
Words of the litany and a reader.

□ *Introduction*

The 1st Sunday in Lent is the traditional time to look at the theme of temptation as we remember the temptations of Jesus in the desert.

During Lent we start to examine ourselves in greater depth in preparation for Easter. The things we do wrong often occur because we give in to temptation, and so before we look at these faults we must look at temptation.

□ *Top ten temptations*

Before the service create a top ten list of temptations for children and adults. Put this up on an overhead projector or board, or make individual sheets for everyone.

A suggested list of temptations might include the following, but you will need to make your own, suitable for your church and locality:

Top ten list of temptations

1. Tempted to eat too much (or eat too much junk food).
2. Tempted to tell white lies (or lie to get out of trouble).
3. Tempted to lose one's temper (or swear).
4. Tempted to put oneself first and others second.
5. Tempted to steal time by being late for work or school (or to 'borrow' things from work).
6. Tempted to drink, smoke or play the computer too much.
7. Tempted not to say prayers, read Bible, or go to church.
8. Tempted to gossip, talk about others behind their back (or tell tales).
9. Tempted to treat some members of society as second-class citizens, e.g. women, ethnic minorities, children, handicapped, homosexuals, etc.
10. (Leave blank)

Ask the congregation to put the list of temptations down in order – with their greatest temptation at the top. So if losing one's temper is someone's biggest temptation they will put No. 3 at the top of their list. No. 10 is left blank for any temptation they may wish to include.

☐ *Groupwork*

Create groups of separate ages. Children's groups may well need someone who will act as an enabler and help the children to come to their own conclusions.

Each group should discuss their individual conclusions as far as they are able. If this proves too difficult, approach the subject by looking at what temptations are generally considered to be the greatest in our society.

The groups may not be able to come to a consensus but the important thing is that discussion takes place about the whole subject of temptations.

When all the groups have come to a natural break, gather everyone back together and ask for some comments from the groups. What temptations do they think are the greatest? Which are the hardest to overcome?

Optional: Group for young children

Younger children could play a game of 'pairs'. Create cards out of pictures cut from duplicate magazines (or photocopy pictures) and paste onto card. There should be at least thirty cards. Temptations may re-occur using different pictures. The temptations could include:

- pictures of children fighting;
- pictures of expensive and desirable toys;
- pictures of junk food;
- pictures of an animal being mistreated.

The pictures will need some explaining before the children begin playing. Then cards should be shuffled and placed face down. Children choose two cards trying to make a pair. When they don't achieve a pair the cards are replaced for someone else to try again. Allow discussion during the game if it occurs.

Optional You might wish to use the whole or part of Psalm 139 during this service to reinforce the idea that God knows how we are tempted. The Psalm could be said with alternate verses from different parts of the congregation, or used as a meditation with accompanying pictures projected onto a screen (e.g. verse 7 = the sky; verse 8 = the sun rising over the sea).

☐ *Conclusion*
Continue by referring to the Old Testament reading (Hebrews 4.12–end) and the Gospel reading (Luke 4.1–13). Jesus was tempted for three days at the start of his ministry, but we are told that he did not give in to the devil.

Comment that God knows all that we are and all that we do. There is no escape from him *but* we have someone who will speak to God for us – Jesus, the Son of God – and he understands how we are tempted, for he too was tempted, even though he remained sinless.

Create a litany of confession on the following lines:

Leader: Lord God, when we are tempted to speak unkindly or spread rumours that cause others pain, help us to be strong.
All: Lord, hear our prayer.

Leader: Lord God, when we are tempted to put ourselves first and not heed the needs of others, help us to be strong.
All: Lord, hear our prayer.

Leader: Lord, God, when we are . . .

2nd SUNDAY IN LENT

The King and the Kingdom: conflict
Christians can never be far from conflict, because the struggle between good and evil is relentless. The congregation are encouraged to see the world as it really is.

Genesis 7.17–end   Matthew 12.22–32

> Newspapers, magazines and scissors.
> Frieze paper or sheets of sugar-paper, and Pritt Stick.
> Strips of coloured sticky paper and pencils.
> Prepared board or a large sheet of cardboard to create a 'rainbow'.

☐ *Introduction*

Speak about the theme of 'conflict'. In the Old Testament reading (Genesis 7.17–end), we see men and women in conflict with God. God is patient but in the end the Maker is inevitably drawn to destroy what he has made. Only Noah and his family are found to be of worth.

In the Gospel reading (Matthew 12.22–32), we are reminded that 'He who is not with me is against me'. Conflict is seen as inevitable in the Kingdom. Good inevitably attracts evil – or shows it up for what it really is!

With God, though, there is always hope – symbolized today by a rainbow.

☐ *Activity*

1. WORLD CONFLICT

Using a large number of newspapers and magazines ask the congregation to go through them to find *headlines* that show as many different kinds of conflict as possible. They might wish to include headlines on the following subjects:

war	arguments with neighbours
rebellion	misunderstandings
family quarrels	law suits
parliamentary arguments	divorce
child molestation	murder
strikes	

Imaginary headings could be written up for those that cannot be found.

Finally stick the cut-out headlines onto frieze paper or large sheets of sugar-paper and hang round the church walls for everyone to see.

2. PERSONAL CONFLICT

While the final pasting of the headlines is being concluded, give out rectangles of coloured sticky paper to each adult and child.

Encourage them to use the slips of sticky paper to record
personal conflicts (small or large), that they may wish healed.
More than one slip can be given to each person, as desired. If
they prefer to keep these anonymous, suggest that they write on
the sticky side of the paper!

Ensure as far as possible that everyone completes this, even if
they write 'I will speak more pleasantly to . . .'.

When all the slips are completed these may be brought up to
the front and stuck down on a previously prepared 'rainbow'
picture or board (a board marked out with curved 'tram-lines'
where the colours are to be placed). Try to encourage everyone to
stick the coloured slips in the appropriate place for a rainbow
colour!

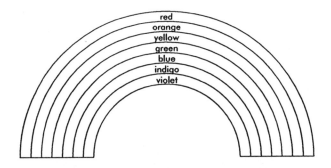

Note: You may consider ill-health to be a sign of conflict.

Put up the rainbow with a suitable heading, and leave the
display up for a few weeks.

☐ *Conclusion*

Conclude this whole section of the service with a short and simple
comment:

'As the rainbow was a sign of hope, and a sign of God's
promise to Noah, so let it be a sign of hope, and a sign of our
promise to God this day.'

 The intercessions could be omitted – as they have already been
offered!

3rd SUNDAY IN LENT

The King and the Kingdom: suffering

All too often we want to live our life our way because God's way is too difficult.

Matthew 16.13–end

> Leaders for the game, freeze-frame drama, and haikus.
> Paper, paints or pencils.

☐ *Introduction: Game*

Play a game of 'follow my leader', making it as difficult as possible. Allow any adults who wish to sit this out just to observe, but do encourage *some* adults to join the children.

Actions to copy might be:

- Arms up; arms down; jump; touch your toes.
- Hop around the church; sit on the floor; pick up three books with one hand; do press-ups.
- Pat your head and rub your tummy with a circular movement at the same time; close your eyes and touch your nose.

Stop the game when you begin to get some 'drop-outs' and allow everyone to sit down again.

☐ *Comment*

The game of 'follow my leader' describes in a fun way what Jesus was talking about in today's Gospel reading (Matthew 16.13–end). He said that if we want to follow him we must renounce ourselves and take up our cross and follow him. By this he meant we should always put ourselves second and God first, and take up a life of sacrifice serving others.

The important thing is *not* that we give up our life for others as Jesus did, but that we serve him in the very small things every single day. Each day we must follow Jesus in our thoughts, our speech and our actions, wherever he leads us, copying all his actions.

☐ *Groupwork*

Inform the congregation that today they are going to look at some of these small ways of putting God first and themselves second. Allow them to choose a group activity.

GROUP A: FREEZE-FRAME DRAMA

Divide into a number of small groups of no more than six adults and children. Each group should choose one of the story-lines below and talk about what it might be like to 'put God first' in this situation.

   a. Living with an elderly relative.
   b. Living with children.
   c. Living alone.

When the group are ready choose one of these examples (for example what an average day with someone elderly could be like) and make four or five 'still photographs' using members of the group as the actors. Lastly and quickly, create a few words that will help explain the story-line or connect the scenes together.

When this is shown to the congregation the narrator asks the congregation to close their eyes as the story-line is read. When the group have 'frozen' into their first 'photograph', the congregation are asked to open their eyes. This is continued for the other 'photographs'.

GROUP B: HAIKUS (SEE 2ND SUNDAY AFTER CHRISTMAS)

Write haikus on the subject of 'Putting God first in my life'. Ensure some discussion takes place before beginning to write the haikus.

GROUP C: PICTURES

Draw or paint pictures to express what it is like to 'put God first'. Discuss at the outset: How do we feel when God wants us to do something opposite to what we desire?

☐ *Conclusion: Plenary*

Come back together and allow everyone to share their work: hang up the haikus and paintings for general inspection, and watch *some* of the freeze-frame drama. Make sure the remainder are watched after the service over coffee, or the following week.

 Create a litany for confession or intercession:

> *Leader:* Father, so often we want to . . . Help us to live our lives *your* way.
>
> *All:* Help us to live our lives your way.
>
> *Leader:* Father, so often we want to . . . etc.

4th SUNDAY IN LENT (Mothering Sunday)

 The King and the Kingdom: transfiguration
The guiding principle for a Christian is love.

Colossians 3.12–17

> A story-teller and a script or notes of the story.
> Flowers or small gifts for 'carers'.

☐ *Introduction*

Comment that although today is 'Mothering Sunday' many people will want to thank whoever looks after them (or who looked after them in the past), whether this is mother, father or aunt. Those whose mothers are dead will also want to remember them with thankfulness.

Add that today you are going to tell a story, not about a mother but about someone who cares for other people. The New Testament reading (Colossians 3.12–17) reminds us that because God loved us we too must love other people. We can show that love by being kind, gentle and patient with others. We must be quick to forgive, generous with others and above all everything we do must be done in a spirit of love.

☐ *Story: Snowy*

● You will need a story-teller – who may or may not be yourself.

- The story should be told from *memory* if possible, and the notes used as a guide. If the story-teller is new at the job encourage them to make up the words if they get stuck, and to keep their eyes on the congregation as much as possible. Good eye contact will ensure those listening keep interested. For this reason the text of Snowy shown below can only be thought of as an indication of how one person would adapt the story-line.
- Encourage the story-teller to practise reading the story into a tape-recorder the week before, and to criticize themselves for pace and pitch of voice.

Notes for Snowy:
- Snowy, a teenager, bakes all morning.
- Mother is in hospital and Dad's at work.
- Next-door-neighbour comes in saying that Bill Harris, a crotchety neighbour, has broken his leg.
- Snowy takes Bill a casserole and he's pleased to see her.
- Snowy gives Mrs Davies a cake for her twins' birthday party.
- Visits Mum in hospital and gives nurses a plate of cakes.
- Her young brothers Ben and Tom eat the gingerbread.
- Next day Snowy takes a quiche to church lunch.
- With no food left all her organization for next week is undone!
- Church presents her with flowers and food for following week, and thank her for her hard work.

Note: Snowy could be a teenage boy!

Snowy

Snowy was hot and tired. She had baked all morning – sponge cakes, egg-and-bacon flans, a casserole, and some gingerbread. The table in the kitchen was laden with food; even the window-sill of the small flat held a plate of cakes cooling. The smell in the room was a mixture of fruit and icing sugar – every adult's memory of childhood.

Snowy surveyed the scene, pleased with her efforts and glad she could stock the freezer for the following week. Indeed the freezer would be overflowing, but at least it would keep the family going till Mum came out of hospital.

'Anyone there?' the voice called, even as Snowy heard the knock on the door and rose somewhat tired to answer the call.

'My, what a lovely spread', said her neighbour as the teenager let her into the small flat. 'You've been busy this morning!'

Snowy smiled, pushing back the lock of white hair that fell across her face.

'I'm just going to have a cup of coffee. Will you join me, Mrs C?' she asked.

Mrs Cameron shook her grey head. 'No! Thanks. I can't stop, I've got to dash. I just called in to ask you to give your Mum my love when you see her, and tell her I'll pop up the hospital tomorrow if George will run me there.'

She smiled at the teenager as she picked up a bun. 'Oh! By the way, Bill Harris has broken his leg. Apparently he fell down the outside step when he was chasing some of the kids. That'll serve him right, won't it?' With another grin she had left.

Snowy began to do the washing up while the kettle boiled, her mind already preoccupied with the old man downstairs. He was always complaining about the noise the kids made and chasing them with his old army stick. Snowy had a run-in with him only a few days ago over absolutely nothing.

It was a shame, for he was all alone. His daughter hardly ever came to see him. Perhaps if she took him the casserole she'd made it would cheer him up, for he must be finding it difficult to manage with a broken leg.

Later, as Snowy set about preparing lunch she thought back over the morning and her visit to Bill Harris.

He'd actually smiled, and seemed pleased to have a visitor. In fact he'd not grumbled once about the kids. Perhaps he was just lonely with nothing else to think about but the kids who clattered up and down the stairs outside his door all day.

Whatever the reason, he'd invited Snowy in *and* eaten some of the casserole there and then. Before long Snowy found herself offering to come in and see him later in the day.

On the way back Snowy had bumped into the twins' Mum. She looked somewhat harassed.

'Hi! Snowy!' she greeted her. 'How's your Mum?'

'Getting better. She should be out in a week or so', said Snowy making room for Mrs Davies to come down the stairs.

'Great! Send her my regards, won't you?' She swung past the girl heading down the stairs two at a time. 'Must dash! I've got to

get to the shops before they close. It's the twins' birthday and
what with one thing and another I've forgotten the cake!'

'I've got one you can have, if you want', said Snowy. The
words were out almost before she knew it. 'You're welcome to it if
it's any help.'

'Any help?' said Mrs Davies coming back up the stairs. 'You're
a life-saver, that's what you are my girl!'

Minutes later the triumphant Mrs Davies bore the cake off to
her flat and the chaos of preparation for the twins' party.

'Come up and join us Snowy, if you can bear the noise', she
yelled back.

Later that day Snowy gave a plate of cakes to the nurses who
were looking after her mother, before returning to babysit for her
younger brothers so that her father could go to the hospital.

Ben and Tom had demolished most of the gingerbread and
gave Snowy sticky grins. She made no comment about washing
hands or faces for they might as well have a 'holiday' while Mum
was away. Normal rules would apply soon enough.

Ben grinned at his older sister.

'Smashing ginger bread, Snow. As good as Mum's!'

'By the way,' said Tom who was nine years old and two years
older than his brother, 'don't forget the lunch at church
tomorrow. I bet Dad's forgotten.' He ducked back under his

duvet and rescued the last piece of gingerbread. 'Aren't we supposed to take something?'

Snowy's brow wrinkled. 'Blast! Never mind Dad! I'd forgotten as well! Oh well I'll have to take the quiche.'

She closed the bedroom door, pulling it sharply for it always stuck, and returned to the kitchen to survey the mess. She wouldn't be sorry to have Mum back. It was alright looking after the family for a few days, but what with GCSEs as well, there seemed no time for herself. All that baking she'd done for next week to save time. She might as well not have bothered.

After the service on the following day the members of St Chad's congregation met in the new church hall for their patronal festival lunch. It was a custom that had started about eight years earlier and was always an event enjoyed by everyone from the youngest to the eldest.

Mum would be sorry to miss the lunch, thought Snowy as she helped the smallest members of the Junior Church up the stairs to the hall, and settled them at one of the long tables.

The room was packed by the time the Vicar stood up to say grace, and there was much fun and laughter during the meal as families and friends chatted and talked. It wasn't often they all met together like this, and they made the most of it.

At last, though, the meal was eaten and the dishes cleared away, and in the lull the Vicar stood up. He paused, looking down the hall at the rows of tables, as though seeking someone, and then cleared his throat slightly.

'Before we close this afternoon with an item by the choir, I have a special announcement to make.' He looked round the hall.

'We have a very special person with us today, someone who deserves a reward. This person has worked her socks off, never complained and has done all this with a smile on her face.' He paused again, a slight smile on his face.

'Snowy, we'd like to give you this with our love.'

In his hands the Vicar held the beautiful bouquet of flowers that had decorated the top table.

Snowy found herself moving up the aisles as people cheered and clapped her affectionately on the back. She was aware of the smile of approval on her father's face, and Tom and Ben's enthusiastic roar. Then she was beside the Vicar.

'And since a little bird has warned me that all the baking you did this morning has been given away, we'd like to give you these.'

As he spoke, the door to the kitchen opened and out came some of the helpers who had been washing up. Their hands were full of plates of food. There were quiches, sausage rolls, cakes, and even a plate of cold meat and salad.

'That should keep the family going for part of the week,' said the Vicar smiling down at Snowy, 'and give you some time off!'

Snowy smiled at them all, overwhelmed by their kindness. What a very strange kind of day it had been!

☐ *Thank you*

Include a time of 'Thank you' in the service, by asking everyone to say the following:

Children:	(to parents/all adults) Thank you for all you do for us.
Men:	(to wives/all women and to children) Thank you for all you do for us.
Women:	(to husbands/all men and to the children) Thank you for all you do for us.
Leader:	Let us offer one another a sign of thanks through a kiss or handshake.

Make sure that everyone in church is included in this offering.

☐ *Conclusion*

Conclude this part of the service by giving small bunches of flowers or presents to the 'carers' in your church who take Christ's message of love to other people through their actions. This may be to mothers (or fathers), or you may wish to thank other people who deserve particular recognition.

Note: If you are going to use the service for the Fifth Sunday in Lent, ensure you ask the congregation to bring photographs of themselves.

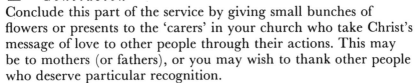

5th SUNDAY IN LENT

The King and the Kingdom: the victory of the cross

Christ died on the cross because of our sins, and we are freed from the consequences because of his sacrifice. The cross is the symbol of our freedom.

Mark 10.32–45

Materials to make a very large cross: planks of wood or a
small tree, and rope.
Plastic sheeting, earth, and rocks.
Wood for small crosses for the congregation, and string.
Photographs of all the congregation, or paper and pencils to
draw themselves.
Pritt-Tack or drawing pins.
A ladder.

☐　*Before the service*
In the previous week create a small-scale 'Golgotha' in church.
Make a *large* cross out of wood, with a base, and stand it on
plastic sheeting. Cover the base of the cross with earth and rocks
to create a hill. Keep the hill bare and 'unfriendly'. It is definitely
not a 'green hill' yet.

Arrange for the congregation to bring photographs of themselves
to the service.

☐　*Introduction*
Remind everyone that it is Passion Sunday – one of the most
solemn days of Lent when we begin to think about the death of
Jesus.
　In the Gospel reading (Mark 10.32–45) Jesus tells his disciples
that when they reach Jerusalem he will be given to the chief
priests, who will condemn him to death and hand him over to the

Romans. He is to be mocked, spat upon, flogged and finally killed. *But*, he says, three days later he will rise again.

☐ *Comment and activity*

THE CROSS AND OUR SINS
Ask all the congregation to join you around the cross.

Comment that the theme for the service is 'The victory of the cross'. This dreadful instrument of death was to be the means for bringing us back to God. In some amazing way, because Jesus willingly offered his life for us, we have been saved from the consequences of our sin.

Refer to the cross standing beside you. This cross stands as a reminder that Jesus went to his death on a cross for each person present. Because of their sin they are separated from God, but Jesus offered his life so that they could be forgiven.

Give out small pieces of wood and string, and ask each person to make a cross for themselves by tying the wood together. Help smaller children as necessary.

When the crosses are finished invite the congregation to stick them into the earth at the foot of the large cross *in silence* as a reminder that Jesus died because of their sin. With every fresh sin it is as though they re-crucify him.

You might want to list some very ordinary and normal sins at this point, for instance: pride, not thinking of others, being selfish, etc.

THE CROSS AND FORGIVENESS
Remind the congregation of the reading. Jesus knew he was going to die, and because he chose this course willingly he succeeded in freeing each person present from their sins. They are forgiven and restored to the loving arms of God.

Now ask everyone present to fix a photograph of themselves onto the large central cross as a reminder that Jesus died for them so that after repentance they are freed from their sins.

Give out some Pritt-Tack or drawing pins and encourage everyone to go over to the cross and fix their photograph onto it.

If someone has forgotten to bring a photograph, ask them to draw a quick sketch of themselves.

Do include photographs and pictures of babies and very young children.

☐ *Conclusion*
Comment that the crosses will stay on the 'hill' until Easter, when they will be removed to create an Easter garden. The photographs

will stay throughout the Easter period as a reminder that Christ died for all people.

 Allow a moment of silence by the cross if possible, before closing with a simple prayer.

PALM SUNDAY

 The way of the cross
Palm Sunday is a time for welcoming Jesus. We also remember that he is to be rejected by these same people a week later.

Matthew 21.1–13

> One or more 'runners' and some primed people.
> A number of men in modern costume, and a donkey if possible.
> One man to act the part of Jesus.
> A child to accuse the congregation.
> Copy of the prayer.

☐ *Introduction*
Arrange for an adult to burst into church through the main entrance doors at this point of the service. They should be out of breath as though running for some time and extremely excited. Also ensure that there are a number of primed people sitting in the congregation who are capable of helping.

Ensure that the 'runner' proceeds to give a message to two or three people at the back of the congregation, asking them to pass the message on.

The message is in fact a rumour and should be given slightly differently to different people. For example:

'The prophet's coming!'
'Jesus, the man who makes the dead live, is coming to our church any minute!'
'Jesus, the Messiah, is coming!'

Ensure by this time that there is a feeling of excitement by asking appropriate questions of the whole congregation as the messages are gradually passed on:

'What's happening?'
'Who's coming?'
'What is it?'

Your primed people should also help to stir the excitement, through their demeanour and voice. This is their primary task.

When the excitement is high enough, Jesus and one or two disciples should enter, with or without a donkey! Preferably these should be adults dressed in modern costume. There could be some women and children in attendance if desired, and they may be talking excitedly together. For example:

'Look at all the people!'
'Where are we going?'
'What are they all looking at?'

If the excitement has been raised to a sufficient height, the congregation should quite naturally erupt into applause, cheering, arm-waving, or other signs of welcome. The primed people should be encouraged to throw service sheets or other suitable paper at 'Jesus', and shout 'Welcome Jesus!' or 'Hurray'. The organ could join in as well.

☐ *Comment: Taking a look at Jesus*
Allow Jesus to make his way to the front of the congregation and to stand where he can be seen by everyone. His head should be bowed and he should remain motionless. His disciples and followers should be standing near, but to one side.

Now ask the congregation to look at Jesus carefully. Then, using a neutral voice – as of a television commentator – make the following observations:

> Here is a young man only in his thirties, a carpenter from Nazareth. There's nothing remarkable about his life. Yet rumour has it that he heals those who are very ill, causes the disabled to run, forgives those who sin, and can make the dead live. Rumour also has it that he is the promised Messiah, the one who comes from God to save us. Look at the way we have greeted him today.

At this point ensure you are interrupted by someone who should join you out front. A child of about twelve years old would be appropriate. Allow them to point out fairly aggressively to the congregation the following facts:

> But in one week's time *you* will not be shouting 'Hurray!' or 'Welcome!', you will all be shouting 'Crucify him'. In one week's time you will kill him on a cross! That is what you will do to the Son of God!

Allow a moment's silence while all the actors freeze in their positions. Finally ask those who have helped you to return to their seats in the congregation.

☐ *Buzz groups and discussion*

Invite everyone to turn to their neighbour and consider why they think the people responded so differently to Jesus on Good Friday. Was it just the fickle attitude of a crowd, or was there more to it?

Children and teenagers might prefer to consider if they behave differently when they are in a crowd or gang.

After a few moments ask both adults and children for some answers.

☐ *Conclusion*

Conclude by pointing to 'Jesus' (who has returned to join you, again motionless and with head bowed), and comment that we too welcome Jesus into our lives, but all too often reject him when the pressure of the crowd gets too much.

 Light a large candle at a central point in the church (or more than one if the church is large) allowing for a moment's silence. Then read the following prayer:

Creator God, forgive us when we destroy the world that you created. Forgive us when we deny knowing your son Jesus Christ and crucify him again by our actions. Forgive us when we doubt the power of your Spirit. We ask this in the name of our Lord, Jesus Christ. Amen.

MAUNDY THURSDAY

The Last Supper
At the Last Supper Jesus initiated our Eucharist or Communion
Service. Today the congregation are encouraged to look at this
whole service in some depth.

Note: Although the Alternative Service Book has been used, other
forms of this service could be used with some small alterations.

1 Corinthians 11.23–9

> An overhead projector or board and paper, and felt-tip pen.
> Two readers.
> Alternative Service Books.
> One Book of Common Prayer.
> A cook with ingredients for a simple meal and the necessary
> items for laying a table.

☐   *Introduction:*
Remind the congregation that there are a number of different
titles given to the *Communion Service* (substitute the name
customarily used in your church, as appropriate). Ask for any
other names and put these up on the overhead projector or board.
   Names most commonly in use:

> Eucharist
> Holy Communion
> Lord's Supper
> Mass.

Unusual titles:

> The Mysteries
> The Action.

Discuss with the children what they might like to call this service,
and don't be surprised if you get some unflattering comments!
These could also be put up on an overhead projector or board.

☐   *Comment*
Comment on the meanings of these words:

 ● Eucharist: Thanksgiving.

- Holy Communion: Used from the Reformation. Prior to this the people did not take much part in the service and rarely if ever took communion. After the Reformation the service became 'common' or open to all people.

- Lord's Supper: Popular with Non-Conformist churches, and very scriptural.

- Mass: Used by the Roman Catholic Church in particular. Derives from the words said at the end of the service in dismissing the congregation: *Ite, missa est.*

- The Mysteries: This title belongs to the Eastern churches where much of the action of the service is carried out away from the people by the priests.

- The Action: Used by the church in Scotland.

☐ *The preparation*

Invite your first reader out:

READER 1: Read the introduction to the Eucharist from the Book of Common Prayer.

Comment that this reminds us that those in open disagreement with one another who have not 'said they are sorry' will not be able to receive communion. It also reminds us that those who wish to receive communion must tell the minister the day beforehand. Although this is out of date it is a salutary reminder of preparation!

READER 2: Read Note 1 to the Eucharist from the Alternative Service Book.

This reminds us that everyone should prepare themselves before they receive communion.

Comment that you will be looking at the importance of preparation, with the help of someone who loves cooking.

Invite your guest to join you. This should be someone from the congregation who is well known for their love of cooking. The person should bring with them the necessary items for cooking a favourite but fairly simple meal, as well as a previously cooked meal, and cutlery and decorations for laying a table.

Allow them to explain (or encourage the answers by questioning them) what ingredients they need for their favourite meal, where they buy these, and how they would cook the meal. Show the congregation the ingredients, and let them see the finished product which will have been cooked earlier in the day. Encourage your speaker to refer to the importance of decorating the table to enhance the special meal. Finally thank them for their help.

Continue by commenting that special meals need special preparation. The Eucharist is a special meal and we should prepare ourselves through prayer and meditation – thinking about those times we have failed to do what God asks of us.

Part of the preparation to receive our special meal, the Eucharist, occurs within the service. At the beginning we are greeted by the host who says, 'The Lord be with you'. Then we are invited to confess our sins (note that sometimes this occurs later in the service), and if we wish, to praise God by using the words of the Gloria.

☐ *The Word*

At the heart of the next part of the service, the Ministry of the Word, are the readings from the Bible. The sermon or talk usually refers to them.

Today's 'sermon' is in fact commenting on the epistle, 1 Corinthians 11.23– 9. You might wish to ask if anyone can remember what that was about!

☐ *The Creed*

Then follows the Nicene Creed. This is our response to the readings and word of God. It was written as a result of the Council of Nicaea in AD 325. There are three creeds.

If possible have copies of the Book of Common Prayer available and allow the congregation to find the three creeds:

- The Nicene Creed: Holy Communion Service;
- The Apostles' Creed: Morning and Evening Prayer;
- St Athanasius' Creed: Alternative creed to be used at Morning or Evening Prayer.

If only the ASB is available the congregation might like to compare the Nicene Creed in the Eucharist with the affirmations used in the Baptism Service.

Now invite the congregation to stand and say the Creed (or the affirmations).

☐ *Prayers of Intercession*

Having been reminded of our duties as Christians, (one of which is to pray for those who need our prayers) we now come to the Intercessions, or prayers for other people.

The Intercessions should now be given by a member of the congregation. Keep these very short and visual this week.

☐ *The Peace*

This is the oldest part of our service. Ask the children how they greet their friends. Then continue by asking different age groups in the congregation. Suggestions might include:

- slap hands together
- say 'Hi!'
- give a kiss
- shake hands
- say 'Hello!' or 'How are you?'

The 'kiss of peace' was part of the Eucharist in AD 150. Nowadays we only shake hands and say 'The peace of the Lord be always with you'.

Add that the people of God are now thought of as being at peace with one another (have forgiven one another) and are now ready to feast together.

The Peace is now celebrated. If you are not accustomed to exchanging the peace with your neighbours – try it!

☐ *Laying of the table*

For our special meal the table must first be laid.

Go through the actions of 'laying a table' (that is, of preparing the gifts). The bread and wine should be brought up from the congregation. You might also wish to put the cloths onto the altar. Explain exactly what happens.

☐ *Thanksgiving*

The great Thanksgiving Prayer which follows reminds us why we celebrate this meal. Do not continue by saying this prayer, but continue to comment about the remainder of the service first.

☐ *Communion*

This is the time when we 'sit down to eat' our meal.

If appropriate, discuss with the congregation what it feels like to have a special meal with the family of God when often half of the family are missing – i.e. the children. Ask the children how they feel about not receiving the bread and wine. How do adults feel if they don't receive communion?

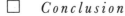 □ *Going out*

After the meal, all that remains is to say 'Goodbye'. The meal is a blessing and a strengthening for service so all that is left is to say thank you to God and to go!

Note that the Dismissal is mandatory, although the blessing is optional, for surely we have been blessed through receiving the eucharist, but we must say 'Goodbye' (or 'God be with you!').

 □ *Conclusion*

Now say the Prayer of Thanksgiving and continue by receiving communion and finally dismissing the people. If possible do not conclude with a final hymn after the dismissal.

GOOD FRIDAY

 The crucifixion of our Lord

The traditional 'stations of the cross' are used to create a meditative all-age service for Good Friday.

Isaiah 53.2–5
Isaiah 53.7–11 (or 53.7)
Matthew 11.28–30
Matthew 27.55–8
Matthew 27.59–61
Mark 15.17–20a
Luke 2.33–5
Luke 23.26
Luke 23.27–32
Luke 23.33–4
Luke 23.44–7
John 19.4–6
John 19.17
Romans 7.21–5
Hebrews 5.7–10

> Paper and felt-tip pens for pictures.
> Paper and pens for prayers.
> Separate slips of paper with each Bible reference and picture title for each group.
> Good News Bibles for those who can read.

□ *Introduction*

Explain to the congregation, as necessary, that the stations of the cross are the incidents that occurred in the last few hours of Jesus' life.

Many churches display pictures showing these incidents and if this is so in your church, explain that you will be using them as the background for a series of meditations and studies of the last few hours of Jesus' life.

If your church has no such pictures then these can be created in the groupwork session, and you will need to explain this to the congregation.

The following are the stations of the cross:

THE STATIONS OF THE CROSS
1. Jesus is sentenced to death. (John 19.4–6)
2. Jesus carries his cross. (John 19.17 and Matthew 11.28–30)
3. Jesus falls. (Isaiah 53.7–11 (or v.7 only)
4. Jesus greets his mother. (Luke 2.33–5)
5. Simon picks up Jesus' cross. (Luke 23.26)
6. Veronica wipes the face of Jesus. (Isaiah 53.2–5)
7. Jesus falls again. (Hebrews 5.7–10)
8. Jesus speaks to the women of Jerusalem. (Luke 27.27–32)
9. Jesus falls again. (Romans 7.21–5)
10. Jesus is stripped of his clothes. (Mark 15.17-20a)
11. Jesus is nailed to the cross. (Luke 23.33–4)
12. Jesus dies on the cross. (Luke 23.44–7)
13. Jesus is taken down from the cross. (Matthew 27.55–8)
14. Jesus is laid in the tomb. (Matthew 27.59–61)

Note: The readings are often symbolic and not actual. So reading No.6 refers to the Christian's responsibility of helping the poor and downtrodden.

□ *Groupwork*

Encourage everyone to opt for one of the groups according to preference, and give the groups a specific time limit to complete their task.

GROUP A: TABLEAUX
● Create tableaux of the different stations of the cross using as

many people and groups as desired. These can then be used
later in the service to accompany the readings and prayers.

- Look up relevant Bible passages and talk about each incident
  as necessary before creating the tableaux.
- Depending on numbers divide the Bible passages and
  tableaux as appropriate.

GROUP B: READINGS

Allocate the different readings to this group and allow them to
practise reading the verses ready for later in the service.

GROUP C: PRAYERS OF REFLECTION

Allocate to this group the task of creating short three-lined
prayers applying each station of the cross to life. For example:

Station No. 5: Simon picks up Jesus' cross:

Lord Jesus, give us the strength and the desire to help
shoulder the burdens of other people, and not to walk by on
the other side.

*Optional
group*

GROUP D: PICTURES

Using the readings and titles for the stations of the cross draw
pictures to accompany them. A number of pictures may be
drawn for each station if desired, otherwise create one large
picture. Work as a mixed-age group or allow individuals to
work alone.

☐   *Conclusion*

Finally bring the groups or individuals back together. Place the
pictures around or outside the church. Then *walk* the stations of
the cross if space permits and using the work from all the groups:
e.g. stop at each picture to hear the reading (from a member of

Group B), pause for a moment to contemplate the tableaux
(Group A), and close with an appropriate short prayer (led by a
member of Group C).

If it is difficult for the whole congregation to move around the
church perhaps the pictures could be held up (or the tableaux
shown centrally) for all to see. However, if at all possible it is
preferable to actually walk the stations of the cross with the whole
congregation, even if this means some will stand on the seats or
pews! Alternatively, if weather permits, walk the stations outside!

Note: It is important to make sure that the 'meditations' are kept
short.

EASTER DAY

Resurrection
The resurrection of Jesus Christ demands absolute faith on the
part of a Christian believer, and calls for a re-examination of
what we mean by 'faith'.

Mark 16.1–8

> Two or three adults or children to speak about things or
>   people in which they have faith.
> Sugar-paper and felt-tip pens.

☐ *Introduction: I have faith*
Inform the congregation that you have invited two or three adults
and children to help the congregation think about having faith.

The speakers should be of all ages and should have been
primed to talk particularly about something which is beyond their
control, and difficult or impossible to understand. Allow them to
speak for about two minutes and to give as much insight,
information and humour as the subject demands.

Suitable subjects
- My heart (or breathing).
- The sun will shine tomorrow.
- Someone loves me.
- My computer.

☐ *Activity: Faith is . . .*
Ask the congregation to work in small informal groups, and give
each group a felt-tip pen and some paper. Their task is to create
as many statements on 'Faith is . . .' as they can.

The statements can either be written on fairly large sheets,
ready to be hung round the church or onto small banner-size
sheets (approximately 60cm × 15cm).

Example of 'Faith is . . .':
- Faith is opening my eyes each day.
- Faith is prayer.
- Faith is reaching out . . .

☐ *Comment*
Having explored a little more the meaning of the word 'faith', we

have seen that among other things it is believing in something despite any other evidence to the contrary. It is also belief in the impossible.

Note that Jesus was crucified and died. Comment that every human being who is born will die! We can all understand this, but what we find difficult to understand with our brains is that Jesus rose from the dead. He defeated death and was seen alive after he was certified as dead.

Refer to the Gospel reading (Mark 16.1–8). The women who went to the tomb were so terrified of the good news that Jesus was alive, when they had expected to find his body ready for the funeral rites, that they ran away. Faith is almost always very difficult for we find it very hard to believe what our rational brain tells us is impossible!

Finally, conclude that Jesus died and rose again so that we could defeat death and be free from our sins. What we have to do is to hold to that faith despite anything our rational faculties may tell us.

□ *Conclusion*

Place the 'Faith is . . .' statements all round the church and allow everyone to walk round and look at them.

Note: If you intend using the service for the 1st Sunday after Easter, you will need to ask the congregation to make a note of the food they eat during one specific day of this next week.

1st SUNDAY AFTER EASTER

The Bread of Life
An investigation of how much bread we need for our body, reminds us of how much food we need for our soul.

John 6.32–40

Overhead projector or board and paper and a felt-tip pen. Notes of food eaten on a specific day by members of the congregation.

> Copies of the loaf picture for all the congregation.

☐ *Introduction: Daily food chart*

Create a chart with the help of the congregation to show how much food they have collectively eaten for a specific day in the previous week.

It might be a good idea if the week before the service the congregation are asked to keep a check on how much food they eat for one day. This could perhaps be put into the parish magazine or handout in order to spread the message to as wide a number of people as possible.

Those who come unprepared can probably work out what they had for the previous day.

Using an overhead projector or board and paper (or a long piece of frieze paper spread on the floor with everyone around it), begin to work out how much food the congregation consumed for one day of the previous week.

Start with bread in slices (say approximately 25 slices to a loaf) and go on to tea, coffee, milk, sugar, eggs and meat. Some of it will be guesswork and you will probably be unable to list all the food consumed. If necessary, end up with some collective groups of food.

Example:

Food Chart for . . .   (date)

loaves

pints

dozen

kg

pks

pks

jars

lb

lb   lb

☐ *Weekly and yearly food chart*
When you have finally worked out some kind of satisfactory food
list for one token day multiply this by seven and then by 52 to get
a weekly and yearly total.

Although both the weekly and yearly total would have a
greater variety of food items it will still give you a good average
intake for a selection of items for the week and the year.

Comment that if we remember that many of us live 70 years at
least, we begin to see the enormous quantities of food we all
consume. We might also begin to see how much of our nation's
work is taken up with producing that food. Ask for suggestions:

- farmers   - advertisers
- fishermen   - banks
- wholesalers   - restaurants
- shopkeepers and staff   - the cook at home

The list can be almost endless. All this to keep us alive!

☐ *Discussion*
Discuss with the congregation how long they have gone without
food at any time in their lives, what it feels like to have to lose a
lot of weight, or put on a lot of weight, and the fads and fancies
we may have over food. What times of the day do people eat?
Are there people who must eat regularly (e.g. diabetics)? Are
there some people who only eat once a day?

☐ *Comment*
Much of our life seems to be taken up with food. If we're not
buying it, we're cooking it or eating it, or trying not to eat it. It is
one of the most important things in our life, even if sometimes we
rather take food for granted.

Refer to the Gospel reading (John 6.32–40) and the importance
of bread (or 'manna') to the Jews. It was believed that just as
God had given them bread to eat in the wilderness, so when the
Messiah came he would give them manna. It was seen as being
one of the signs that would point to someone being the Messiah.

Comment that Jesus turns the people's question on its head.
They have been looking for the wrong kind of bread, he says. *He*
was the bread of life.

97

Refer to the food chart created earlier, and add that just as we saw how badly food was needed to keep the body alive so we need Jesus to keep our soul or spirit alive! We are not just physical creatures, we are also spiritual creatures, and as much as we need food for the body we need food for the soul. Jesus says that he will give us food for eternal life.

□ *Prayer activity*

Give everyone a picture of a small loaf of bread (a simple outline picture like that above will do) and a pencil. Then ask them to work with the people close to them to decide in what way Jesus gives them food for eternal life.

Some suggestions might be:

- peace
- forgiveness
- love
- stillness.

Allow each person or group to come to their own decision on what food they receive from Jesus.

Ensure that children are helped to see that we are not just physical creatures, but that we are also spiritual beings that need inward sustenance.

Finally ask everyone to write down their conclusions on the picture of the loaf of bread as a reminder of the spiritual food they receive. Suggest that they take the picture home and use it to continue thinking about the gifts they receive from Jesus.

□ *Conclusion*

With everyone standing and holding their picture of the bread say the following prayer:

Father, for this spiritual food that you have provided, may we be always grateful. Amen.

Sing 'I am the bread of life' (MP)

Note: If you are intending to use the service for the Sunday after Ascension, and invite outside speakers, this will need to be done now.

2nd SUNDAY AFTER EASTER

The Good Shepherd
Jesus said that he was the Good Shepherd. We are reminded of
what these words really meant in the Palestine of 2000 years ago.

Ezekiel 34.7–16   John 10.7–16

> A modern-day shepherd and some sheep, or a group of
>   children dressed as sheep with masks, some teenagers
>   dressed as wolves with masks, and an adult to act as the
>   shepherd with a crook.
> Chairs to create a sheepfold if desired.
> Copies of questions or information on shepherds in Palestine.
> Copies of Anthony de Mello's poem if desired.
> Frieze-paper, felt-tip pens, crayons, or paints as desired.

☐ *Introduction*
Explore the theme of the Good Shepherd by choosing either of
the following options.

OPTION 1
If your church is in or near the countryside try to find a farmer
who would be prepared to bring two or three sheep into the
church or churchyard, and then allow themselves to be questioned
about their work. Weather and numbers permitting, you might
wish to continue outside with the congregation gathered round
the farmer.

Allow the congregation to ask questions of the farmer. For
example:

- How many sheep do you possess?
- Where do you keep them?
- Do they always live outside?

- How many lambs did you have this year?
- Do the sheep ever try to escape?
- Are the sheep difficult to look after?
- Do they get sick often?
- What food do the sheep like to eat?
- What natural predators do sheep have?

Note that sheep are not easy creatures to look after even today. They continually try to escape, and suffer a variety of illnesses. Encourage the farmer to give a true picture of shepherding.

OPTION 2
If Option 1 is impossible, create your own shepherd and sheep. Dress a number of small children in white clothes and masks (see template on page ...) to act as sheep, and an adult in suitable costume can become the shepherd. Don't forget a crook!

Finally, build a wall, possibly out of chairs turned inwards, to act as a fence, and place the sheep inside. Use the questions above in Option 1 as the basis for questioning this fictional shepherd. The shepherd will need to be familiar with the information about sheep below.

SHEEP

'Sheep are animals looking for reasons to die'

Sickness:
- When sick they stand with head down, ears are flat, eyes sad, they walk badly and look miserable.
- They are prone to problems with their feet and skin; parasite worms in the stomach; and attract flies which lay their eggs in cuts or abrasions, thus the sheep begin to breed maggots.
- The most dangerous illness is sheep scab which is a notifiable illness causing flocks to be destroyed.

Prevention:
- Sheep are dipped in July as the hot weather comes in against fly maggots, and again in the autumn against sheep scab.

Breeding:
- Sheep breed earlier and earlier. Their breeding cycle is governed by the length of the day – the shorter the day the more virile they become.

- Many lambs are now born before Christmas.
- Normally lambs are born as the grass begins to grow – in March.
- Gestation period is 21 weeks.
- Between 50% and 60% of ewes in a flock will have twins, and about 10% triplets.
- Approximately 10% of a flock is kept for breeding and the rest is sold for slaughter or breeding.
- Wool is almost worthless. Australia, for instance, has approximately 20 years of global stock.

Food:
- Sheep eat fresh grass, dried grass, hay, straw and concentrated corn with added minerals.

☐   *A shepherd in Palestine*

Begin to talk about shepherds and sheep 2000 years ago in Palestine. Comment that when Jesus was alive the shepherd had a hard and dangerous life. He spent his whole time caring for the sheep, finding them fresh pasture and water, and keeping them safe from natural predators.

Explain how the shepherd protected his sheep: circular pens were built with no door or gate. The shepherd would lay down in the open doorway to keep the sheep in and the wolves out. He protected the sheep with his body.

The work of a shepherd was also lonely as the shepherd was often away for months at a time searching for the freshest grass in the mountains and hills. It was cold because the temperature at night in the mountains often fell to freezing, and it was dangerous, for as well as wolves there were snakes, scorpions and even robbers.

The good shepherd coped with all this for the sake of keeping his sheep healthy and safe. The sheep grew to know his voice, and followed him wherever he led them, while he searched for those who went missing and rescued them from crags and cliffs, often carrying them back on his shoulders to the safety of the flock.

Finally, comment that in the Gospel reading (John 10.7–16) Jesus said that he was both the door to the sheepfold and the Good Shepherd, and that we are all his sheep.

Optional | The comment above could be accompanied by mime if desired. Use chairs turned inward to act as the sheep pen and a man dressed in appropriate Palestinian costume as the shepherd. Dress small children as sheep and teenagers as wolves. Use the templates on page ... to make masks.

☐ *Buzz groups*

Ask the congregation to turn to their neighbour for a moment and make any comments.

After a moment or two encourage the congregation to ask themselves the following questions:

- What has Jesus done to protect and look after me?
- What kind of a sheep am I: lost, being carried back, safe in the fold, terrified, content?

Optional | 1. You might use this poem by Anthony de Mello:

> *A sheep found a hole in the fence*
> *and crept through it.*
> *He wandered far*
> *and lost his way back.*
>
> *Then he realized that he was*
> *being followed by a wolf. He ran*
> *and ran, but the wolf kept chasing*
> *him, until the shepherd came*
> *and rescued him and carried him*
> *lovingly back to the fold.*
>
> *In spite of everyone's urgings*
> *to the contrary, the shepherd refused*
> *to nail up the hole in the*
> *fence.*
>
> (from *The Song of the Bird*, New York:
> Image Books, 1981)

De Mello calls this poem a 'parable for educators'. It could be used as a basis for discussion involving questions like, 'Do we need to be open to danger if we are to have free will?' and 'Can God really protect us at all times?'

2. You may wish to create a frieze. Half of the frieze could show the life of a shepherd in Palestine 2,000 years ago as it really was. The other half of the frieze could show Jesus as the Good Shepherd protecting us and keeping us safe. This latter might include physical protection from accidents or death, provision of food and drink, or spiritual protection.

 Preface the intercessions with 'Great shepherd of the sheep'.

Note: If you are intending to use the service for the Sunday after Ascension the invitations to speakers will need to go out shortly.

3rd SUNDAY AFTER EASTER

The Resurrection and the Life
Human beings are both physical and spiritual creatures but St
Paul reminds us we should set our minds on higher things.

Colossians 3.1–11

> Dark and light shirts or tops, and candles and matches if
> desired.
> Bibles for Group B and paper and pencils.
> A quiet room for Group C to use and a copy of the
> meditation script.
> A large candle and matches for Group D and some paper
> and a pen.

☐ *Introduction*

Remind the congregation of the two sides of human nature – the
physical and the spiritual – by reading the first verse of the New
Testament lesson (Colossians 3.1) again.

Comment that St Paul says we are both physical *and* spiritual
beings. We have bodies but we also have feelings and ideas, and
imagination. However we frequently seem to be controlled by our
body. For instance, when we are talking to God in prayer we may
well become aware of our stomach and of how hungry we are!

Jesus came to rescue us from being slaves to our bodies and to
the things of this world, and to show us there is a better way to
live. Today, therefore, the congregation will be exploring this
whole theme of the physical and the spiritual in a variety of
different ways.

☐ *Activities*

Offer a variety of different groups and encourage all the members
of the congregation to join one of the activities.

GROUP A: MIME AND MOVEMENT

This group should aim to produce a piece of mime or
movement to illustrate the words 'The physical is death and the
spiritual is life'.

Spend a moment or two discussing the theme before
beginning to mime or dance.

Some suggestions which might be helpful are:

103

- Light and dark themes could be explored, in which case it would be sensible to have some dark and light shirts or tops available.
- Candles could be used in order to express some aspects of the spiritual.

- If the group is fairly large consider dividing into two allowing one group to portray the physical and the second the spiritual.

GROUP B: BIBLE STUDY

- Re-read the first four verses of the New Testament lesson (Colossians 3.1–4) and discuss what these words say to each member of the group.
- What does St Paul mean by 'your life lies hidden with Christ in God'? And how does the group think 'we will be manifested with him in glory'? How does the group think we can allow our thoughts to dwell on a higher plane when we have to live a day to day existence in a world that is very secular?
- List some sensible ways of being 'spiritual'.

GROUP C: GUIDED MEDITATION

This groupwork will only be possible if there is somewhere quiet for the members of the group to work.

Allow the members to sit or lie down. Go through a relaxation technique:

Firstly, close your eyes ...
Wriggle your toes ...
Stretch your arms and relax ...
Circle your head on your neck ...
Stretch your fingers and relax ...
Stretch your whole body as much as you can, and relax ...

When the members of the group are completely relaxed continue by using the words below:

Be aware of your body . . .
The weight of your head . . .
The pressure of your feet inside your shoes . . .
The feel of your clothing against your body . . .
The pressure of your skin . . .

Become aware that the 'essential you', your 'spirit', is within this body . . .
Your spirit is free . . .
Your spirit is gentle and kind . . .
Your spirit is at peace . . .
Your spirit is in tune with God . . .

Allow your spirit to speak to your body . . .
What does it say . . . ?

Then, when you are ready come back to the present,
aware that you can always get in touch with the spiritual inside
yourself again . . .

Discuss what happened in the Guided Meditation and the effect it may have on each person's life during the coming week.

GROUP D: DISCUSSION GROUP
Place a large lighted candle in the middle of a circle to act as a focal point for the discussion.

Consider the thought that Christ died for us so that we might live. At our baptism we said (or our Godparents said on our behalf) that we were made one with Christ in his death and in his resurrection. Create an explanation of these ideas suitable for an eight-year-old child to understand, or explain to any children present what this means.

The group might want to consider what they think Jesus did for us and why he did this, also what happens at our baptism. Look up the words in the Baptism Service if desired.

☐ *Conclusion*
Gather everyone back together and hear from the different groups. The mime and movement group could present their offering at a later point in the service.

4th SUNDAY AFTER EASTER

The Way, the Truth and the Life
Jesus reminds us that we must have trust in God. The congregation are helped to see what this means by using 'trust' games.

John 14.1–11

> Five hard-boiled eggs and one 'blown' egg in an egg box.
> Two volunteers and a chair.
> An umbrella.
> Paper and pencils for optional activity.
> Biddings for prayers.

☐ *Introduction: Game*
Use one of the following games as a way of introducing the theme of trust in God:

GAME 1
Start with six eggs in a box. Five eggs are hard-boiled and one should be a 'blown' egg. Place one chair in front of the congregation and invite two volunteers to come forward. You may wish to prime these people before the service.

Ask the volunteers if they trust you. Hopefully they will reply 'yes'. Inform them that there are five hard-boiled eggs in the egg box, and one that is 'not hard-boiled'. Allow everyone to see the perfectly normal-looking eggs.

Invite one of the volunteers to sit on the chair, suggesting that you wish to break an egg over their head. Check with them that they still trust you and offer them the use of an umbrella should they prefer.

Break one of the hard-boiled eggs over their head. Then invite the other volunteer to sit down in their place.

Continue breaking the hard-boiled eggs over their heads, but offering them the use of the umbrella each time. Reiterate 'You're sure that you still trust me?' periodically. The blown egg is the last to be broken.

Whether the last volunteer chooses the umbrella believing the final egg to be raw or trusts you to the end, does not matter. Simply adjust your comments accordingly. (This game is based on an original idea by Sue Toogood.)

GAME 2

Invite a group of people to join you and to carry out a knee-sit. The group should stand in a very close circle, one behind each other like sardines. At a given moment the whole group sits on the lap of the person behind them. The group should not collapse!

GAME 3

Invite seven people to join you. One should lay down on the floor and close their eyes. This person is then gently lifted off the floor by the six other volunteers.

Use seven new volunteers and repeat the game if desired.

Alternatively invite at least fourteen adults to join you and stand in pairs in a line, one behind the other. Then ask if anyone trusts the group. Choose a volunteer and ask them to stand at the front of the line, with their eyes closed. They are then lifted gently, over the heads of the pairs until they reach the back of the line. This can be done a number of times with different volunteers.

Optional activity Either in groups or as a whole congregation, create a list of situations in life where it is necessary to trust in someone.

Example:

birth	the dentist
babyhood	hospitals
a marriage partner	that the dustmen will call
that play-time will occur	

Optional discussion Discuss with the congregation, or as buzz groups, whether it is easier to trust in someone when you are a child. What do the children think of this? Does it get harder to trust people and situations as we get older? How does this apply to trusting in God? Do children have anything to teach adults about trust?

☐ *Comment*

In the Gospel reading (John 14.1–11), Jesus reminds his disciples that they are to trust in him and in God. If they know Jesus then they also know God. The questions and the worrying all disappear when we have trust in someone, all that we need to do is to follow and obey them.

Refer to the trust games, as desirable, either because the volunteers did not trust you, or because they did.

☐ *Conclusion: Prayer*

Conclude by holding hands in a huge circle (or by joining hands at the ends of rows), and say a prayer that you have specially created for the service. The prayer could be responsorial with a refrain:

Leader: Lord of all trust, help us to . . .
All: Lord, our trust is in you.
Leader: Lord of all trust, help us to . . .

Note: If you are intending to use the service for the 5th Sunday after Easter, ask the congregation to come the next week with thoughts concerning people whom they no longer see. Young children should bring their favourite cuddly toys. You may also need to ask members of the congregation to speak, for the Sunday after Ascension.

5th SUNDAY AFTER EASTER

Going to the Father

Separation cannot divorce us from God's love, just as physical separation of distance or death cannot stop us loving someone.

Romans 8.28–end

Group leaders.
Young children with cuddly toys.
Sugar-paper, crayons, felt-tip pens and Pritt-Tack.

☐ *Introduction*

Inform the congregation that they will be looking at what it means to be separated from someone or something that we love. Comment that you hope it will not be upsetting for anyone, and that those who understand what being separated is like will feel able to help others to understand that love continues despite any distance involved.

Add that only when we understand human relationships can we understand God's love for us.

☐ *Groupwork: Activities*

The previous week you should have asked the congregation to think about people they love who are now separated from them by distance or death, or because they have lost touch with them. Young children should have been asked to bring their favourite cuddly toy.

After your introductory comment separate the congregation into different groups. You will need to appoint some group leaders. Young children should remain as one group with two or three adults.

GROUP A: CUDDLY TOYS (YOUNG CHILDREN)

Talk about the cuddly toys the children have brought and discuss those left at home. How long have the children had them and who gave them? Do they sleep with them, and have they ever been lost? What happened then? (Be prepared for some long-winded stories on the day the teddy got left at Grandad's.)

Note: Some children may have the same affectionate feelings for comforters in the shape of pieces of material or blankets.

Discuss with the children whether they would feel the same for their cuddly toy if it were outside the door, or at home, or at Granny's, or indeed lost. Get them to see that they would love their toy wherever it was, even if they never saw it again.

Mention that just as when they are away from their cuddly toy they still love it, so when they are away from Mum or Dad (like now or when they go to playgroup or school) they are still loved.

Comment that it is the same with God. We may not be able to see him (though we can see the things he does in the world), but he never stops loving us.

Create a poster headed 'God loves' and place all the children's names below. Alongside the children's names you may wish to get them to put a drawing of their cuddly toy, reinforcing that as they love their toy so God loves them.

GROUP B: DISCUSSION (OLDER CHILDREN AND ADULTS)
This group(s) should be of no more than six people. Allow each person a moment or two to reflect aloud on someone they love who is no longer with them. This might be a parent or partner who has died, someone they have lost touch with, a favourite pet who is dead, or a relative or friend who has emigrated. What do they remember best about them?

Continue by discussing whether distance or time have affected their love. Comment that the New Testament reading says that even though Jesus returned to be with God the Father, 'Nothing can separate us from the love of God in Christ Jesus.'

Does the group believe this? Do they think, for instance, our behaviour might affect God's love for us? (For example if we murdered someone – or said we didn't believe in him?)

GROUP C: POETRY (OLDER CHILDREN AND ADULTS)
As a group, brainstorm words concerned with the character of someone they have lost. Write all the words down onto a sheet of paper. Try to keep the brainstorming to about three minutes and be as positive as possible. Reject nothing, but encourage the group to keep their thoughts on the loved one and *not on their own feelings*.

When the group have completed the brainstorm encourage them to write poetry or haikus (see 2nd Sunday after Christmas) about the person from whom they are separated.

Comment that God feels the same about us, and encourage some of the group to write poetry in the voice of God about his separation from us. Note that he still loves us!

GROUP D: DANCE OR MIME
Discuss what it is like to love someone you cannot see any
more. Do our feelings change? Do we ever stop loving them?
Do we only remember the good times?

The New Testament lesson says God loves us like this and
that we can never be separated from him. Show this in mime
or dance.

☐ *Conclusion*
Hold a plenary session to hear back from the groups. Use the
mime or dance, and possibly some of the poetry later in the
service. Show the children's poster and put it up somewhere in the
church for a week.

Finally comment on how the love of God transcends time and
distance: God simply loves us!

Note: If you are intending to use the service for the Sunday after
Ascension you will need to ask people to speak on their different
gifts.

ASCENSION DAY

Leaving the disciples
The return of Jesus to his heavenly Father meant that the
newly-created church had to continue growing in strength.

Matthew 28.16–end

> Adults to talk about children growing up and teenagers who
> will talk about leaving home.

☐ *Introduction: Talk*
During the previous week find a number of adults willing to talk
about allowing children to grow up. Either ask them questions or
invite them to stand up and speak.

Questions that could be asked:

● Did you find it difficult to let your children make their own
mistakes?

- How did you manage to stop doing everything for them?
- When did you have to step in and pick up the pieces?
- What did it feel like when they left home?
- What was the hardest thing about allowing your children to grow up?

Optional 1. You could invite someone to speak about letting a child or adult with special educational needs cope on their own. In this instance the parent or adult often has to be cruel to be kind and allow the handicapped person to fall over or hurt themself in the interest of allowing them to stand on their own feet. How difficult is this? Often it is easier to do things for someone who maybe slow, rather than let them finish the task for themself. What problems does this create?

2. Ask some teenagers or young adults to say what it felt like when their parents or guardians withdrew their help. How did they manage to live without money from parents; what was it like having to do all the washing and cleaning? Would they wish this transition period to be in any way different?

3. You might also wish to ask a younger child when they intend to leave home, and what job they hope to do. How do they think they will manage while they are training or out of work? Be prepared for some odd answers.

☐ *Discussion: A helping hand*
Question the adults in the congregation on how they helped their children to manage for themselves the first time they had to leave them–perhaps for a weekend, or a week.
What strategies did they use:

- cooking to fill the freezer;
- leaving phone numbers where they could be contacted;
- telling neighbours they were away;
- doing their washing when they returned home;
- giving them extra money.

Optional Look at ways in which we are like teenagers or children trying to manage on our own away from God our Father. What sort of mess do we make of living things our way, and what do we get right?
 Use newspapers and magazines to help decide these questions and collectively begin to write the intercessions for the day.

☐ *Conclusion*
Comment that Jesus must have felt like a parent watching his children struggle on their own. Yet he knew he had to leave the

disciples and go back to be with his Father. Unless he left they would always rely on him to help them, instead of solving their own problems for themselves.

Jesus' last act is to give the disciples authority (i.e. permission and power) to go and tell the world what God has done for them. Then like any good parent he leaves his contingency plans: they will wait in Jerusalem to receive the power of the Holy Spirit!

SUNDAY AFTER ASCENSION

The Ascension of Christ
The church is given gifts to equip it for its work in the world.

Ephesians 4.1–13   Luke 24.45–end

> A variety of people willing to talk about the work they do for the church, or a number of people from other denominations who will talk of the traditions and customs in their church.

☐ *Introduction*

Comment that one of the hardest things the disciples ever had to do was to let Jesus go. At his death they were bewildered and scattered – rather like lost sheep. Then came the amazing news of the resurrection which gave them renewed confidence. But within a short time they were faced with the prospect of having to stand on their own two feet when Jesus returned to his heavenly Father. Jesus said this was vital if they were to receive the power of the Holy Spirit.

This was not the only gift the new Christians were to receive. In the New Testament reading (Ephesians 4.1–13) St Paul reminds us that we have been given a number of gifts to continue the work of building up God's church: some people are apostles, some prophets, some evangelists, some pastors, and some teachers.

Explain that today the congregation are going to spend time looking at what some of these people do in 'our own church'.

☐ *Activities and talks*

Prior to this service invite a number of people to think about the work they do for the church, and ask them to share their thoughts with the rest of the congregation. Be as imaginative as possible and choose people who may not think of themselves as 'prophets' or 'pastors', but who are nevertheless doing God's work in this way.

People with some of these 'gifts' might include:

- Bible study group leaders
- the vicar or minister (or lay reader or deacon)
- sick visitors
- secretary to the PCC / church governing body
- street wardens
- any Christian who is known to be good at listening or counselling
- choirmistress.

Ask *all* these people to share the work they do with others in the congregation. Encourage the congregation to gather round the speakers in small groups and ask them about the work they do for the church. Encourage the speakers to bring visual aids: e.g. books used with children, or other items appropriate to the work.

Invite the congregation to ask questions. For instance:

- What do you do?
- How do you do it?
- How long have you been doing it?
- Did you have any training?
- What books or resources do you have to help you?
- Why do you do it?

If any of the speakers find it difficult to talk about their work suggest they think back over the period of a week or a day, and simply tell people what they have been doing.

Allow the congregation to go to more than one person, as desired.

Optional Local Ecumenical Projects or churches working closely with other denominations might like to invite adults and children from a number of denominations to talk about their faith and their church.

They could look at the different emphases in worship, and the different traditions and customs. They might also want to explain about their different histories and how this particular denomination came about. Where possible invite the speakers to bring items to be examined by the congregation: a rosary, wafers, thurible, individual glasses for wine, etc.

Try to encourage the congregation to keep the questions as positive as possible so that the guest speakers do not feel pushed into a corner.

Conclude by thanking God for the rich variety of church life and witness. Also attempt to include some flavour of the different denominations in the rest of the worship.

☐ *Discussion*

Gather the congregation back together again and discuss the question of 'Where are the prophets?' (Should you have found prophets, but not evangelists, etc., then change the discussion as appropriate.) You may well have found apostles (that is, preachers), evangelists (those who take the good news to others), and pastors and teachers, but how many prophets did you find?

Prophets are those who interpret the will of God and announce or predict things to come. They are inspired by God to warn and teach. Did you find many prophets? Do we need prophets today? Or are prophets merely seen as negative influences?

Comment that we do not always look in the right places for prophets. Did you find any children blessed with these gifts, and if not, why not? Was it simply because you never thought of looking?

Finally, explain that prophets, evangelists, pastors and teachers need to be in tune with God. They do not speak for themselves but always out of their deep relationship with God.

☐ *Conclusion*

Comment that the Christian church has always been blessed with men, women and children with gifts that enhance the life of the church. With these and the power of the Holy Spirit we can work to build up the body of Christ – that is, the church.

 Include prayers for those people who have been given the gifts mentioned by St Paul, or prayers for Christians of other denominations.

PENTECOST

 The coming of the Holy Spirit
The Holy Spirit is seen at work throughout the Bible not just at Pentecost. The congregation are encouraged to find out more about him and his power.

Exodus 19.16–25   Acts 2.1–11 (or 1–21)

Note: Read the New Testament lesson after the activity.

> Sufficient Bibles for at least half the congregation.
> Sheets of paper or card with Bible references.
> Overhead projector or board and paper, and felt-tip pens.
> Flame shapes and pens, if desired.

☐ *Introduction*

Inform the congregation that today they are going on a 'Holy Spirit' hunt. They are going to search the church for Bible references, and then search the Bible for evidence of the Holy Spirit to discover what activities he engages in. This will be done before hearing the New Testament reading which tells of the coming of the Holy Spirit to the disciples at Pentecost.

It might be worth reminding the congregation that the Holy Spirit – the third member of the Trinity – is a 'he' and not an 'it'!

☐ *Activity: Holy Spirit hunt*

Prior to the service make more than enough cards or slips of paper for the whole congregation and write a Bible reference on each one showing a *different aspect* of the Holy Spirit. You may wish to duplicate readings for a large congregation.

Use both the Old and New Testaments, endeavouring to show the whole range of activity engaged in by the Holy Spirit. Some suggestions might be:

Genesis 1.1–2	Exodus 31.1–3	1 Corinthians 12.3–13
2 Samuel 23.2–5	Judges 3.10	2 Corinthians 1.21–22
Psalm 139.5	Judges 14.6	Galatians 5.16–25
Matthew 12.25–32	Psalm 51.10–12	2 Peter 1.20–21
Matthew 28.18	Isaiah 11.1–3	John 15.26–7
John 14.15–17	Isaiah 32.14–18	Isaiah 63.10–14
Isaiah 42.1–4	Acts 5.1–13	John 3.5–8
Ezekiel 36.26–7	Acts 20.28	2 Corinthians 3.15–18
Romans 8.9–11	John 14.25–6	Acts 1.6–8
John 16.7–15	2 Corinthians 13.13	Romans 5.1–5
Ephesians 4.29–31	Acts 11.16–18	
Romans 8.1–27	1 Corinthians 2.1–13	

Before the service hide the slips of paper or card all round the church, making sure they are placed at different heights – taped under chairs or pews, behind flower vases and on window ledges. Ensure some can be found easily and some are more difficult to find.

Give out Bibles and ask the congregation to search for the slips of paper. Preferably this should be done in twos and with mixed age groups.

Having found a Bible reference they should look it up and read it together. Finally they should try to decide what aspect of the Holy Spirit the reading shows. For example, Psalm 139.5 would show the range of the Spirit's power – he is everywhere at all times. Romans 5.1–5 shows that he is the means of transmitting God's love to us.

If some complete this activity fairly quickly send them out again to look for another Bible reference.

ptional | References suitable for younger children could be placed on different coloured card and hidden in suitably low places, if desired.

☐ *Conclusion: The characteristics of the Holy Spirit*

When everyone has completed the activity and as many references have been found as possible choose one of the following two options:

1. Ask a number of adults and children to share with everyone what they have discovered about the Holy Spirit.

2. Use an over-head projector or board and paper and put up as many different characteristics of the Holy Spirit as the congregation can define.

Comment that with greater understanding of the Holy Spirit the congregation are now ready to hear the New Testament reading about the coming of the Holy Spirit at Pentecost.

 Offer prayers of intercession 'in the power of the Holy Spirit'. Or give out flame-shaped pieces of paper and encourage people to write their own prayers.

Note: If you are intending to use the service for the 3rd Sunday after Pentecost initiate a collection of tin cans (size 450 grams) today.

TRINITY SUNDAY

The Trinity
The great mystery of the Holy Trinity is examined through the words of some of the greatest of the trinitarian hymns.

John 14.8–17

> Hymn books or copies of chosen hymns for each group.
> Group leaders.
> Dictionaries.
> Large sheets of paper and pens or felt-tips for each group.

☐ *Introduction*
Comment that the great mystery of the Trinity is not one that we can easily put into words. Over the centuries hymnologists have struggled with the meaning of the Trinity – of a God who is three yet one. Today the congregation is going to examine some of the hymns sung at this time of the year to learn more about the Trinity.

☐ *Groupwork: Hymn study*
Create small groups composed of people of similar ages, and allocate group leaders. Then give each group a hymn (or part of a hymn) and ask them to look at what the words *actually mean*.

Dictionaries will probably be needed in order to work out the meaning of words like 'Godhead' or 'ineffable love'.

Any of the following hymns would be suitable:

Father of heaven, whose love profound (A&M/A&MNS)
The king is among us (MP) (suitable for children's group)
Father most holy (A&M/A&MNS)
Holy, holy, holy (MP/A&M/A&MNS)
Holy, holy, holy is the lord (MP) (children only)

Encourage everyone to talk about their understanding of 'the Trinity'. To this end groups might like to try and write down what the words of the hymns mean to them.

☐ *Activity: A picture of God*
When everyone has discussed the subject sufficiently, ask the group as a whole to carry out one of the following tasks:

- Draw a picture that shows your idea of the Trinity. Note that this is what *the group* think about the Trinity, and the finished result should be one picture.
- Mime the group's idea of the Trinity.
- Create some dance or movement on the theme of the Trinity, and put it to one of the trinitarian hymns.

☐   *Conclusion*

Hold a plenary session to hear back from the groups regarding their understanding of the Trinity, and try to see as many pictures and mimes as possible. Use the dance later in the service.

Finally, challenge the groups to go away and write some new trinitarian hymns for next year!

The intercessions could be accompanied by the group's pictures of God, for 'eyes open' prayer.
Or, prayers could be written prefaced by 'Father', 'Jesus' and 'Holy Spirit'. Light candles as each is said, at a focal point in the church.

Note: If you are intending to use the service for the 4th Sunday after Pentecost you may need to contact different missionary societies for display material. See the back of the book for addresses.

2nd SUNDAY AFTER PENTECOST

The people of God
Christianity implies community and in community all are equal and all are valued. A simple demonstration is used to show this truth.

Acts 2.37–end

> Coloured sticky-paper strips – at least one for everyone in the congregation.
> Pencils.
> Two or three adults and children to gather up and present the broken chain.
> Bowl.
> Prayers of confession.

☐ *Introduction*

Arrange for everyone to receive a strip of coloured sticky-paper as they enter church at the start of the service.

☐ *Comment*

Speak about being 'Christians in community'. We are not Christians alone. It is almost impossible to be a Christian alone, for God calls us to live and work together and we have to learn about being a Christian within the community. Alone we can do little – we are simply not effective.

Comment that in the New Testament reading for the day (Acts 2.37-end) we see that the members of the new church lived together in close fellowship. They shared all they owned, allocating to each what was needed, and giving the remainder to the poor. Much of their time was spent in praise and worship, as new Christians joined them daily.

☐ *Activity: Paper chain*

Focus the congregation's attention on the strip of paper they were given at the beginning of the service. Give out more strips and pencils as necessary.

Ask for suggestions as to the paper's use: Is it a bookmark, or a piece of paper for a small shopping list? Comment that on the other hand it's a little floppy for a bookmark, and a little too small for a shopping list. Finally, if no one guesses help them to see that the strips would also make a paper chain.

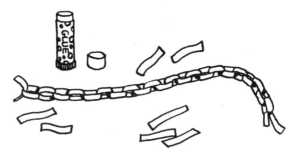

Give out pencils as required and ask the congregation to write their name on their strip of paper. Then encourage everyone to join up their link with their neighbours' to make a paper chain. Ideally, everyone should follow their link, wherever it goes – 'because the glue may come unstuck'.

General confusion will prevail, and indeed the links may not hold so that people will physically have to hold the joints together. However, wait until the chain is as complete as possible and everyone is touching some part of it before you continue.

☐ *Comment*

We are rather like these small pieces of paper. We are neat shapes and pretty colours, but not much good on our own! However together we can create something – just like the paper chain; we can create the kind of church that God wants.

We are only as strong as our weakest link. At this point ask one person to step back and break the chain. Comment that when one of our community is unhappy or ill, it is not just their problem, it is a problem for everyone, for the community is damaged just like the broken paper chain.

Then ask everyone to step back *one* step and break the chain. Comment that when we all pull away from each other and do our own thing then the church community cannot remain whole. It requires all of us to 'hold·the links' together, and work at creating something beautiful.

☐ *Conclusion: Music*

Before returning to their seats ask the congregation to sing 'Bind us together, Lord' (MP and JP). This need not be organized as an 'official' hymn and should be sung unaccompanied. The first verse is sufficient.

Note: To make the chain large enough for everyone to hold you might want to add more links. This might ruin the symbolism, but you could treat the links as members of the church past!

Ask two or three adults and children to gather up all the broken links of the chain. Place in a bowl or plate and offer in silence at the altar during the prayer of confession. Leave there for the rest of the service.

Alternatively offer one-line prayers concerning the brokenness of the world, the church and our lives. Close each prayer with suitable words:

Leader: Lord of all wholeness
All: Heal our brokenness.

Note: If you are thinking of using the service for the 5th Sunday after Pentecost you may need to contact missionary societies regarding speakers or hire video or other material. See the back of the book for addresses.

3rd SUNDAY AFTER PENTECOST

The church's confidence in Christ
Jesus is the keystone of the Christian's life, and our lives should be based on him.

Deuteronomy 8.11–end   Acts 4.8–12

A collection of tin cans.
One tin can covered in bright coloured paper.
A table.
'Brick' paper, and pencils.

☐ *Introduction*
Comment that the theme for the service is the 'church's confidence in Christ'. In the New Testament reading (Acts 4.8–12) Peter reminds us that Jesus is like a stone that is thrown away only to be found later as the keystone of the building – the foundation stone which the whole house rests upon.

You might wish to use the word 'brick' to explain the idea to the children present.

Offer to show the congregation what St Luke means.

☐ *Demonstration: The key can*
Prior to this service you will need to have initiated a collection of aluminium cans. They will need to be of a similar size and shape (for example, cans holding 450 grams), and all the cans will need to be rinsed and have their tops removed or taped down.

Ensure that one can is covered or painted in a totally different colour. This is the keystone (or 'corner-tin').

Place a table in front of the congregation and explain that instead of using bricks to make a wall you will be using cans!

Now proceed to act out the New Testament reading (Acts 4. 11) by placing the cans on the table and building a wall. Request some help from the congregation (though ask them to stand behind the table so that they don't block the view of the rest of the congregation), and make sure that both adults and children are included.

Start by placing the keystone down first at a *corner*, and add cans on either side. Balance the second row in traditional brick-layer fashion with each can resting on the two cans below. Ensure that at least one or two cans are rejected for some reason (bent, wrong shape, rusty, etc.), and continue until all the cans have been used up.

ptional You might decide to collect the cans as part of a recycling programme, and approach schools and uniformed organizations for help.

□ *Comment*

When the 'wall' is completed comment that the most important can in this wall is the first one – the key can (or keystone), upon which the others have been placed.

Remind the congregation that Jesus is like one of the cans you rejected as not being up to standard. The people rejected him, but God has made Jesus the keystone – the most important one of all upon which all the others rest.

If our lives are based on the teachings of Jesus and we try to live a Christian life, then we are like a strong and solid wall. But if we reject Jesus and do not place him as the keystone and most important part of our life then we are like these cans!

Take away the key can and ensure that the whole wall of cans collapses.

Continue by referring to the Old Testament reading (Deuteronomy 8.11-end). It is not good enough just to turn to

God when things go wrong. God should be there in our lives at all times, so that we are 'God-biased' (or 'God-based') in everything we think and do.

☐ *Activity: The keystone in our lives*
Give everyone in the congregation a piece of 'brick' paper (that is, a sheet of A5 paper with a photocopied picture of a brick on it) and a pencil.

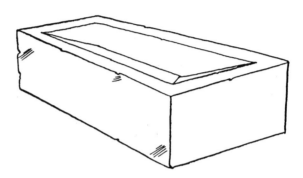

Now ask the congregation to visualize the rest of their day, (or the next one), with Jesus as the foundation stone of their life. Is there anything they would wish to change about themselves or their plans?

For example:
● What will I do this afternoon? (E.g. Have a sleep, clean the car, play outside?)
● Will I now change this and do something else? (Visit someone, spend time with a member of the family, help someone else?)

This task could be completed alone or discussed with a friend or with members of the family.

Adults will need to talk this through with children who are present, but try to ensure that the adults still have time to complete their own thinking.

Request everyone to write down any resolutions they may make on their 'brick'. (*Note*: It is not mandatory to write down a resolution. Inform the congregation that the information on the 'bricks' will remain confidential. Make sure that you dispose of them by shredding or burning them.)

Optional groupwork For those who may wish to pursue this subject further, set up a number of groups to look at any of the following:

1. How can surplus family money be disposed of along

Christian lines (e.g. a holiday in Greece versus using it to help other people).

2. How can surplus church money be disposed of along Christian lines (e.g. a new prayer book for the altar, or more money for mission work).

3. How can we cope with personal failings like a quick temper, pride, envy, or covetousness, in the light of inviting Jesus to be the keystone in our lives?

4. Produce a mime showing how the Christian overcomes the seven deadly sins. Make it as realistic as possible, and announce each sin by using a placard noting its title. Alternatively, carry out this mime with seven different groups.

☐ *Conclusion*
Arrange for the 'bricks' to be collected in and offer these at the altar.

 Use a suitable prayer asking that we may place Jesus in the most important part of our life and act accordingly.

4th SUNDAY AFTER PENTECOST

 The church's mission to the individual
Christians are called to take God's message to other people. The Christian has a responsibility to see that others know the good news of Jesus Christ.

Acts 8.26–38   Luke 15.1–10

> 6–10 messengers and messages.
> Names of simple tunes on paper and some children, if
>   desired.
> A large number of invitations.
> Covenant forms.
> Envelopes.
> Group leaders.
> Display material from missionary societies, if desired.

☐   *Introduction*

Invite a number of people of all ages (between six and ten unless your congregation is very large) out from the congregation and give them all a slip of paper with a task on it. Each task should be slightly different.

Examples of some of the tasks:

- Go and tell someone that *you know well* something you have learnt about Jesus.
- Go and tell someone *you know slightly* something you have learnt about God.
- Go and tell someone *you don't know* what is the most important thing for you about God.
- Go and tell someone *you know well* something you like about being a Christian.

Ask the messengers to carry out the tasks as described, and then give the slip of paper to the people they have chosen. These people now become messengers and should continue with the task. The original messengers should sit down where they are, and not return to their own places.

Children or adults who cannot read will need the instructions interpreting, and very young children should carry out the activity with a parent or other adult.

Don't worry if the noise level becomes fairly high, and stop the activity when all the congregation have been involved.

Optional game   Invite children to go to different members of the congregation and tap the rhythm of a tune to them. It might be the rhythm of 'Three blind mice' or 'Happy birthday' for instance. When the adult has got the tune they are to join in by tapping the rhythm of the tune.

The child sits in the adult's place while the adult goes to someone else with another tune. If someone is unable to identify a tune, the person tapping must keep trying different tunes until one is understood.

☐   *Comment*

Comment that God calls us to do one thing at a time, that is, he calls us to work where we are, with individual people. We are all to be missionaries, taking God's message to individual people in the same way as we have just done.

Refer to the New Testament reading (Acts 8.26–38), and to Philip who was called by God to speak to the Ethiopian. Philip didn't know what to say to the man but God helped him, just as he helped you today by giving you courage and helping you to find the right words.

Add that the Gospel reading (Luke 15.1–10) shows the woman who has lost a coin and the shepherd who has lost a sheep, searching until they have found them. God is just as concerned over each person who does not know him and who is lost, and he expects us to help in that search.

☐ *Groupwork*
- Create mixed-age groups and allocate group leaders.
- Ask the groups to decide what kind of help they can be to God in this work. How can each member of the group best help him?
- Group leaders will need to encourage members to help identify their strengths. These might include:

  - being a good listener.
  - being a good talker.
  - enthusing others.
  - making friends.
  - attracting others because of a happy personality.
  - praying for others.
  - being able to ask others to come to church.
  - a good teller of stories.

- Encourage everyone to identify *one* thing that they could do this week to take God's message to someone else.
- Give out covenant forms and urge everyone to fill one in, making sure that the covenants made are within the capability of each person. For instance, children might wish to ask friends to come and join the choir or Sunday school. Mums could resolve to ask someone to attend the mother and toddlers service. Older people might decide to read the Bible to someone who is house-bound, or to a child.

I ....
PROMISE TO ....
....
....
THIS WEEK IN THE SERVICE
OF JESUS CHRIST

- The forms should then be put into envelopes with the name of the person on the front and the date the covenant was made.

Optional | Hold a display of the work of the different societies concerned with spreading the gospel.

- The Society for Promoting Christian Knowledge (SPCK)
- The Church Missionary Society (CMS)
- South American Missionary Society (SAMS)
- United Society for the Propagation of the Gospel (USPG)

For further information regarding their addresses see the back of the book.

□ *Conclusion*

Offer the covenants at the altar with a suitable prayer. Note that the covenants should be reclaimed in one or two weeks' time, as they are completed.

 Include prayers for missionary work and missionary societies.

5th SUNDAY AFTER PENTECOST

 The church's mission to all men
The church's mission is to tell all people throughout the world about Jesus, for until this happens God's kingdom cannot truly occur.

Luke 10.1–12

> Overhead projector or board and paper, and pens.
> A dictionary if desired.
> Speakers as desired and material from SPCK, CMS, USPG or SAMS.
> Videos or slides as desired.
> Material for any project being initiated.

□ *Introduction: Defining the terms*

Use an over-head projector, or board and paper, and brainstorm the word 'mission'. (That is, ask people to say whatever words occur to them when thinking of 'mission'.) You may wish to use one or two scribes to write up the words.

Note that for many people the word 'mission' is frightening. It is associated with 'evangelism' and they can find it threatening. Therefore allow all the personal hang-ups to come out and make no comment on the words given.

When all the words have been put down try to come up with one or two phrases, or sentences, that describe what the congregation mean by the word 'mission'.

Make a particular attempt to include the children, and create a definition that makes sense to them as well as to the adults.

Example of a definition:

- Telling people Jesus (or God) loves them.

Optional | Brainstorm the word 'evangelism' before looking for a definition. Finally look up the meaning of 'evangelism' in a dictionary.

☐ *Groupwork*

Choose *one* of the following areas of church work and examine it in greater depth:

- Education abroad
- Education at home
- Work with new Christians
- Street evangelism.

EDUCATION ABROAD.

You might wish to look at the work of a society working in the field of education: SPCK, CMS, USPG or SAMS, and invite a speaker or use a slide show or video to look at their work.

Alternatively, if you are involved in sponsoring a child's education abroad through a charity, now might be the time to update the congregation on this project.

Or you could use this time to initiate a new project. For instance, give out Smartie tubes to collect 5p coins to help fund educational projects abroad supported by SPCK; or plan to sponsor the education of a child in the Third World; or arrange to collect old Bibles for IBRA (address at the back of the book).

EDUCATION AT HOME.

Look at the work that is being done by the church in the field of education in this country. Contact the National Society for information, and for slides or videos regarding their work in education.

Alternatively, invite an RE teacher to speak of religious education in school today showing that RE is no longer confessional but is educational. Involve the local Primary School in this if possible.

Or, invite the head teacher of a church-aided school to speak about the church's involvement in education, and explore how the links between church and school can be strengthened. Look at this from an adult and a child's perspective and ask how the adults and children in your church can help strengthen the links.

WORK WITH NEW CHRISTIANS

Use this opportunity to look at work being done in your area among new Christians, for example, a baptism training course or children's nurture programme.

Alternatively, highlight the Sunday school or junior church, or look at work among teenagers. Use people from these groups to talk about them if possible and include pictures or music or drama.

Or, initiate a new programme: set up a baptism training scheme; create a new nurture scheme for young people; initiate a training course for adults working with new Christians.

STREET EVANGELISM

Commission some workers to initiate a street or beach evangelism ministry.

Initiate a new programme of neighbourhood visiting and invite a speaker to talk about this work.

Alternatively, explore the whole subject of street evangelism to see if it might be appropriate for your church to engage in.

Plan a Christian holiday club for children.

Optional | You might wish to use this opportunity to follow up local initiatives started as a result of the Decade of Evangelism.

☐ *Conclusion*

Conclude by a reminder of your definition of 'mission', and if necessary of 'evangelism'. Comment that Jesus says in the Gospel reading (Luke 10.1–12) that 'the crop is heavy, but labourers are scarce'. There is plenty of work for all of us to do if God's kingdom is to come closer still.

 Centre prayer around your project and use the information concerned as appropriate.

6th SUNDAY AFTER PENTECOST

The new man
The Christian is a new person who is no longer tied to the power
of death and darkness. He or she can walk in the light of
freedom.

Mark 10.46–end

> Scarves to bandage eyes.
> Overhead projector or board and paper, and felt-tip pens.
> Invite a blind person to help, if desired.

☐ *Introduction*
Ask the congregation to close their eyes and instruct them to
imagine that they are blind. What difficulties do they imagine
might occur when they go to church, and what things might they
miss?

After a few seconds ask them to open their eyes. Then write up
answers on an overhead projector or board.

Suggestions might include:

Difficulties attending church
● Inability to sing any of the hymns that aren't familiar.
● Knowing where to sit.
● Difficult to get to church.
● Can't see visual parts of the service.

Things they might miss
● Being able to see the church.
● Being able to see friends.
● Reading the hymns and Bible.
● Seeing colours, windows and symbols in church.

Optional | Invite a blind person to speak about their handicap. Ask them to
describe the difficulties *and* the joys of being blind. What is it like
for them to be a member of the congregation?

This will need very sensitive handling and some unexpected or
uncomfortable comments must be expected. Don't excuse what
the church may get wrong, but endeavour to initiate change to
accommodate people with special needs.

☐ *Comment*

The person who is blind cannot stride out freely in case they fall. They must always test and check their way. They live in a world without colour and visual beauty. They may smell a flower, but they cannot see its exquisite colour.

Refer to the Gospel reading (Mark 10.46–end) and Bartimaeus who was blind. All he could do was to shout for help. But when Jesus appeared we are told he 'sprang up and came to Jesus'.

Comment that the story of Bartimaeus the blind man is also symbolic. (See 3rd Sunday after Epiphany for more about symbols.) We are like Bartimaeus until we find Jesus. We stumble along in the dark until we meet Jesus. Then he makes us free to run and leap, and see new sights. It is just as though he has given us new eyes.

Our life after we meet Jesus should be as different as Bartimaeus' must have been after he regained his sight.

☐ *Activity: The new person*

Ask the congregation to create a list of short, pithy sentences to indicate what they think this new person should be like.

If desired, hold a buzz session first to allow ideas to develop and then ask individuals to write up their conclusions on sugar-paper, using felt-tip pens.

Example:

Happy!	Grateful.
Peace-loving!	Forward looking!

Optional activity for young children Gather the younger children together if desired, and tell them the story of *Waterbugs and Dragonflies* by Doris Stickney (Mowbrays 1984). Although this is about death and resurrection, on another level it is a lovely story of new life. Don't try to explain the story, just tell it!

☐ *Conclusion*

Hang the sentences or words all round the church and allow everyone time to look at them all. Leave them up for at least a week if possible.

 Use the list of sentences as a basis for prayer.

7th SUNDAY AFTER PENTECOST

The more excellent way
The congregation are encouraged to see that they are all
following in the way of Christ, by going on a treasure hunt.

Romans 8.1–11   Mark 12.28–34

> Two or three stewards to send and receive groups, and some
>   answer sheets.
> Copies of clues.
> Paper and paper chase leader, if desired.
> Bookmarks or other gifts, if desired.

☐ *Introduction*

Ask the members of the congregation if they have ever been on a
treasure hunt or car rally, where everyone has to answer clues in
order to get to the end of the course.

Discuss what treasure hunts and car rallies are like for those
who may never have experienced them. Explain how often one
clue will lead to the next, and what can happen if you go wrong
on the second clue.

Ask if any of the older members of the congregation have been
on a paper chase, or hare and hounds trail. Explain that these are
no longer possible because there is a penalty for creating litter,
though perhaps an edible trail would be possible!

Refer to the theme for the day, the 'more excellent way'.
Comment that just as in a treasure hunt or paper chase we are
given clues to help us find the right way, so in our Christian life
we are also helped in a variety of ways to find the path that Jesus
wants us to travel.

*Optional
starter:
per chase*
You might prefer to start this section of the service by some kind of
paper chase throughout the church and its environs. The one
difference being that everyone who finds a piece of paper must pick
it up!

☐ *Treasure hunts*

Offer the congregation an option of two treasure hunts,
encouraging everyone to go treasure hunting to see if they can
find the right way to follow.

TREASURE HUNT A

This hunt will probably be carried out inside the church.

Before the service starts place clues on appropriate church furniture. Ensure that they are placed underneath chairs as well as on top of window-sills or cupboards. The tallest and shortest of the congregation must be catered for! Encourage people to work in small groups, with adults answering any questions that may come from the children.

Give clue 1 to each group, with the instructions that when they have solved the clue they should go to the place indicated in the answer. Here they will find the next clue. Continue in the same manner until the end. The answers will need to be held by a number of leaders, to help lessen any catastrophe.

Clues

1. We start here. (Answer: Font.)

2. Tell each other what happened at your baptism, then follow where small legs go. (Answer: Sunday school or junior church area, either inside or outside the church.)

3. Tell each other who first taught you about Jesus, then go where life is received. (Answer: Altar rail. Churches without an altar rail will need to amend this instruction.)

4. Those who have been confirmed, tell each other when this happened and where, and answer any questions asked of you. Then explore where light is shed. (Answer: The lectern Bible, or equivalent.)

5. Tell each other your favourite passage or Bible story, then search where further light is shed. (Answer: A prayer book or stained-glass window depicting something from the life of Jesus, or perhaps a picture of Jesus, or a copy of the ten command- ments if these are displayed around the walls of the church.)

6. Tell each other what one thing you find difficult about the Christian life, then look for the symbol of all our Christian lives. (Answer: A cross.)

7. Tell each other what you think is the most important thing about Christianity, or make a group decision about this. Return to the person leading the service (or sit down).

Optional | You may wish to award everyone with a bookmark, or a card carrying a text emphasizing that our treasure is in heaven, and that when we follow Jesus we are on the right path.
Give out answers to the treasure hunt clues if necessary.

TREASURE HUNT **B**

This hunt will be carried out outside the church. You will need to tailor some of the clues to fit your own environment. Copies of the clues should be held by a few 'stewards' whose job it is to give the groups their next clue when they are ready.

People should be encouraged to work in small groups. It might be helpful to appoint group leaders who will enable the group to talk to each other, but keep an eye on the time!

Give the first clue to each group. The answer to that clue will lead them to a specific place, where they will receive the next clue from a steward.

Clues

1. Where you enter each week. (Answer: Church door.)

2. Tell each other where and when you first entered a church, then go to the oldest Christian remembered. (Answer: The oldest gravestone in the churchyard, or possibly the oldest living Christian.

3. Tell each other who first taught you about Jesus, then find a most important item for the new Christian. (Answer: Water – preferably a stream, or tap. Otherwise the group will have to return inside the church to the font.)

4. Tell each other what happened at your baptism, then find a Christian symbol . . . metres . . . (give direction, e.g. south-west) from here. (Answer: A cross. You may need to place a cross somewhere outside (perhaps made from two rough pieces of wood tied together), to keep the groups outside the church.)

5. Discuss why this symbol is important to each of you, then find an important element of a symbolic Christian food. (Answer: Bread or a baker's, or a cornfield. You may need to place some corn outside.)

6. Tell each other where you were confirmed and when, as appropriate. Answer any questions that children or uncon- firmed adults may have, and then proceed to where we find nourishment together. (Answer: The church.)

7. Tell the others why you go to church and what you best like about it. Then return to the person leading the service (or sit down).

☐ *Conclusion*

Comment briefly, that all Christians are following in the way of Jesus Christ. Some people have just started their journey, and some have been travelling for a long time.

In the Gospel reading (Mark 12.28–34) Jesus reminds us that we must love God and our neighbour. As we have seen, our journey has been much influenced by the people who helped us on our way, for instance at baptism and confirmation.

Comment that perhaps God is calling us to help others on their journey.

Note: Sing 'The journey of life' (CP) or 'One more step along the world I go' (JP).

8th SUNDAY AFTER PENTECOST

The fruit of the Spirit
Sometimes we need to spend time considering the talents God has given us, and helping each other to see that these can be used for the glory of God.

1 Corinthians 12.4–13   Luke 6.27–38

> Overhead projector or board and paper, and felt-tip pens.
> A prepared list of all the jobs in the church that need doing,
>   or prepared sheets for all the congregation (with 'talents'
>   on one side of the page and 'workers' on the other side).
> Rosettes or badges, if desired.

☐   *Introduction: Buzz groups*
Ask the congregation to think of all the things they are good at and the natural talents they may possess, and discuss them with a neighbour. Encourage people not to be too modest.

For example:

- being a good listener
- good at playing the recorder
- understand cars
- can cook.

Allow the congregation to talk about their talents with their family or friends for a moment, and then ask each person to choose one thing from their list. What do they feel is their main talent in life? Younger children may need to be helped to express their talents, and these could include 'good with Granny' or 'being happy'.

Ask different members of the congregation to share their choice with each other, or ask their friends or family to say what they think is that particular person's special talent. Don't push people who may want to keep their thoughts secret.

☐ *Comment*

Comment that all of us have different things we are good at doing. The New Testament reading (1 Corinthians 12.4–13) says that these are gifts of the Spirit. They are given us by God and because of this we should use them in his service.

The reading also reminds us that our church is like a body, and we are the arms, legs and eyes of that body. Each of us, no matter how small we are, is very important to that body. (After all, our fingers are small, but we would find it difficult to manage without them!)

Now choose *one* of the following options to demonstrate the need for the talents or gifts of all the congregation.

☐ *Option 1: The workers*

Use an over-head projector or large board and paper, and write the name of your church in the centre of the page.

Ask the congregation to help you identify *all* the jobs done in your church, and who does them. Add the initials or Christian name of each person alongside the job. For example:

St Mary's Church

THE WORKERS

● cleans (Sue, Rob)	● flowers (Jane, Dave, Mary, Liz)	● types (Chris)	● preaches (Jeff, Jane)
● bells (Don, Bill, Allan, Joe, Pat)	● choir (Jen, Mike, Ann, Fred, Frank, Di, Rose, Zoe)	● grass (Dawn, Adrian, Pat, Bill)	

Be as imaginative as possible to include every small job. When the list appears complete, ask the following questions:

- Does this list of workers represent a large or small percentage of the congregation?
- Are all the different ages represented in the list of workers: children, teenagers, young adults, middle-aged, elderly?
- Are there others we can, or should, include in the list of workers?

Close by thanking all those who do the work, and asking everyone to think about their own talents. Is there any job they could do? If the survey has thrown up any imbalance in who does the work (for instance, the children and teenagers are not involved) can this be rectified, and does a group need to be set up to ensure this happens?

☐ *Option 2: Talent and offering chart*
Create, and then duplicate, a 'talent and offering chart'. Each person will need a copy. On one side of the sheet list all the talents, natural gifts and experiences that are possible, and on the other the work that needs doing in the church to achieve the task that Jesus gave to his church. At the bottom of this second side leave space for people to fill in their names and addresses and one job (or more) that they may wish to offer.

Example (first side):

TALENTS CHART

listener	teacher	knits	driver
good at admin	social worker	types	repairs cars
likes walking	preacher	happy	can bricklay
good with children	an electrician	sings	

Example (second side):

CHURCH WORK

choir	admin	reader	accounts
cut grass	teach	verger	lead services
committee work	study group leader	Sunday school	clean
flowers	visit	key holder	
sick communions			

Name:
Address:
I wish to help with:

Spend time considering what talents each person has and ask them to tick these on the sheet. Can these be offered to the church? Do not pressure anyone but allow them to offer what they feel is suitable.

Collect the forms in and offer at the altar. Ensure that the offers are taken up as far as possible. If it is felt that some people have offered for unsuitable jobs careful negotiation will be needed to ensure that their offer is accepted, but in some modified way.

☐   *Option 3: Awards*

You might wish to highlight certain jobs (or all of them) within the church and officially thank those who do them. Make sure children and teenagers are included.

Create your own award system, perhaps by using badges or rosettes. Then call each person out and award them a 'Thank-you badge'. Try to keep the whole event secret before the service.

☐   *Conclusion*

Close by reminding the congregation that everyone has received some gifts of the Spirit, it is just a question of seeing that the right use is made of them.

Note: If you are thinking of using the service for the 10th Sunday after Pentecost, you will need to begin preparing information about a local or famous person for a 'This is your life' programme.

9th SUNDAY AFTER PENTECOST

The whole armour of God

The word 'Christian' does not mean a 'person who is good'. We are not asked to be supermen or women, just followers of Jesus Christ doing the best we can.

Mark 9.14–29

> A 'Christian Superman'.
> A copy of Bunyan's *Pilgrim's Progress* or *Miles and the Computer* by Taffy Davies.

☐ *Introduction: Sketch*

Dress an adult up as 'Christian Superman' with football shorts over tights, a bright vest, and his initials (CS) written on paper inside a diamond shape and fixed to his chest.

Arrange for him to 'zoom in' fast from outside the church, in typical Superman fashion. As he makes to run past you endeavour to stop him and conduct the following interview, ad-libbed if possible.

You could ask someone else to take the part of 'the leader', but it would be more effective if you could do the part yourself.

Leader:	Excuse me . . .?
Superman:	(impatient) Yes . . .!
Leader:	(a little nervously) It's Christian Superman, isn't it?
Superman:	(breezily) Yes, it certainly is! Can I help?
Leader:	Well I've always wanted to meet you . . .!
Superman:	Nice to meet you! (beginning to leave) I must be off, souls to save and all that.
Leader:	Please, don't go! There's so much I want to ask you!

Superman:	Well, fire away – time is souls you know!
Leader:	(rather stuck now) Er ... how do you do it?
Superman:	Do what?
Leader:	Be such a great Christian.
Superman:	Well it's kind of natural, you know. (rattling off at great speed) Believe in God, never doubt, pray at least two or three times a day, love everyone, do what you can to help others, and follow Jesus' commands to the letter!
Leader:	(speechless) Wow!
Superman:	(about to leave) Right, if that's all, I must be on my way ... !
Leader:	No! Don't go! Tell me, don't you ever get fed up with it?
Superman:	(puzzled) No! Can't say I do. Never enough hours in the day to do God's work, really.
Leader:	Don't you want to say 'Hold it, God! I want to do something else tonight – be a little wicked, maybe?'
Superman:	(shocked) Definitely not! Far too much work to do for God to take time out!
Leader:	And don't you ever doubt it all?
Superman:	No! Can't say I do. It's so obvious isn't it?
Leader:	(very doubtfully) Is it?
Superman:	Well, if that's all. I must go – so much to do!
Leader:	Oh! Well it was nice meeting you. Maybe I'll see you around some day!
Superman:	Quite possibly! Must dash – souls to save, you know. (rushes out)

☐ *Comment*

Ask if this is the congregation's idea of what a Christian should be like – the Christian Superman? Do they think 'Christian' means 'perfect person'?

Today the Gospel shows us a man who wants Jesus' help (Mark 9.14–29). Despite himself he thinks Jesus can cure his son, but has to add 'Help me where faith falls short!'

Comment that the Christian is someone who doubts, gets it wrong, makes mistakes and often has little faith. Christian merely means 'a follower of Christ'. Most of us are pretty bad Christians, but we're still Christians. Jesus helps us where our faith falls short.

Comment that we're not Christian supermen and we don't have to be, because we have a God who forgives us when we get it wrong and starts us again on the right path.

☐ *Story*

Read the story of Christian and Pliable as they fall into the

Slough of Despond, from Bunyan's *Pilgrim's Progress*. Pliable turns back, but Christian is finally given a hand by Help. You might wish to paraphrase the story if the language is considered too difficult for children. It will also need some introduction to put it in context.

Or tell the story of *Miles and the Computer* by Taffy Davies (Scripture Union 1987). Miles uses his computer to scramble the town road-traffic system, but is subsequently forgiven.

☐ *Conclusion*

Comment that we worship a God who understands our human frailty, who forgives us when we're truly sorry, and lets us start again. We are not Christian supermen or superwomen; we are just Christians.

Note: Sing 'Spirit of the living God' (JP).

10th SUNDAY AFTER PENTECOST

The mind of Christ

The congregation are encouraged to use their powers of observation to learn more about each other and about Jesus.

Luke 7.36–end

> Option 1: 'This is your life' subject, book and guests.
> Option 2: Information on one or more famous people, and witnesses to speak for them.
> Facts about Jesus sheets for all the congregation.
> Bibles.

☐ *Introduction: This is your life*

Introduce the theme of 'The mind of Christ' by carrying out a 'This is your life' programme along one of the following lines.

OPTION 1

With the permission of a member of the congregation organize a 'This is your life' programme based on them.

Invite relatives and friends of the person concerned to give information about the person: their Christian life, their birth, baptism and confirmation.

Include such events as their wedding and comments from work colleagues, if this is appropriate.

Endeavour to use as many information-gathering techniques as possible to find out about them:

- letters
- pictures
- memories
- videos

Do include some human weaknesses, as well as gifts and strengths, and try to inject some humour. You might like to give them a 'This is your life' book as a memento of their courage in allowing the demonstration to happen.

OPTION 2
Establish a portrait of a famous Christian person. Find out as much as possible about them, and produce 'witnesses' who will speak about their character and life.

Try to choose someone who is living, although this is dangerous since they may be human enough to let you down one day, but it will speak volumes to younger people in establishing that saints are in the making now.

Again attempt to produce evidence as to the kind of person they are through different media – newspaper reports, books, videos, pictures, etc. Also try to look for their good and bad points.

☐ *Comment*
Comment that we can only know Jesus Christ through what we observe of his life. In the same way that we have learnt about (whoever you have been looking at) through their friends, through letters and reports, so we can apply these techniques to the life of Jesus Christ.

☐ *Bible search: The mind of Christ*
Create individual sheets prior to this service for all the congregation. They should be headed 'Facts about Jesus':

Facts about Jesus

Name	Luke 1.30–32
Town of birth	Luke 2.4–7

Baptism	Matthew 3.13–15
Age	Luke 3.23
Mother's Name	Matthew 13.55
Brothers	Mark 6.3
Job	John 3.2; 17.1–4

Examples of his love for people:

....

....

Examples of his teaching:

....

....

Examples of his love of God:

....

....

Encourage the congregation to work in twos (preferably adults and children) to find out the facts about Jesus. Give each couple a Bible to look up and read the facts. Then ask them to find some examples of his love for other people and for God, as well as examples of his teaching.

Gather everyone together at the end of this session to hear the results from as many people as possible.

☐ *Conclusion*

Comment that our theme was the 'Mind of Christ'. Although we have only touched upon this subject, we have begun to learn something more about Jesus. We have started to see why he acted as he did, and what he has to teach us about living as a Christian.

Use St Richard of Chichester's prayer that starts, 'Lord Jesus Christ, redeemer, friend and brother'.

Note: Sing 'May the mind of Christ our saviour' (JP).

11th SUNDAY AFTER PENTECOST (or Harvest)

The serving community

By experiencing wealth and poverty the congregation are encouraged to see that being the serving community brings with it great responsibilities.

Matthew 20.1–16

> Meal A: Sufficient crispbread or dry biscuits for one-third of
> the congregation served in an old tin, and chocolate
> biscuits or cake for the remaining two-thirds served on
> plates and/or napkins, OR
> Meal B: Overhead projector or board and paper, and felt-tip
> pens.
> Two people dressed as waiters.
> Jug of dirty water, handful of rice and a chunk of bread.
> A copy of *Patterns for Worship*.

☐ *Introduction*

Inform the congregation that today you are going to offer them a meal (real or pretend) to eat in church. Then choose one of the following options:

OPTION 1: MEAL A

Give two-thirds of the congregation no more than one-third of a very plain, stale, piece of crispbread or biscuit, or a small piece of dry bread. Serve this out of an old container or bin and allow them to divide the contents among themselves.

Give one-third of the congregation two chocolate biscuits or a piece of cake each. The chocolate biscuits or bread should be given out on plates and/or napkins, and served elegantly by one or two people dressed as waiters.

OPTION 2: MEAL B
Use the overhead projector
or a board and paper to
write up two menus. Menu
A is for an imaginary
Sunday meal in Great
Britain, of at least two
courses. Menu B is for an
imaginary Sunday meal in
a third-world country.

Menu A: Chicken, roast potatoes, carrots, peas and cabbage.
Gateau and cream.

Menu B: 1 cup water, 1 small handful of rice, 1 small piece of
bread.

Inform two-thirds of the congregation that their meal for today
is Menu B, and one-third of the congregation that their meal
for today is Menu A.

Whichever option you choose you might also wish the two parts
of the congregation to separate to emphasize their wealth or their
poverty. Place a display of flowers near those who are wealthy,
and treat them with deference. Treat those who are poor in a
totally different way.

☐ *Discussion*
Whichever meal you use, discuss with the congregation what it
feels like to be one of the majority or the minority. Did the rich
feel embarrassed? How did the poor feel watching the rich get
more than they had? What about the different ways and different
attitudes in which they were treated?

☐ *Comment*
Look at the Gospel reading (Matthew 20.1–16). Comment that
the landowner chose to treat the labourers as more than equal,
and paid those who only did one hour's work the same as for a
whole day.

Add that we too are called to treat others in our world as *more than equal*. Two-thirds of the people living in our world have too little to eat, and one-third have too much.

*tional* Use any of the following suggestions to look at this subject in greater depth.

- Spend a few moments reviewing what your church does to help others in the world. Decide whether this is sufficient, and whether you can increase the giving. Would it be more efficient to combine all efforts into one particular project?
- Ask someone to come and speak about a new project starting in your area to help the homeless or those who are out of work.
- Initiate a new project to help others. Contact Christian Aid for ideas and projects that need sponsoring. (See back of the book for addresses.)
- Give up one meal this week and offer the money to charity.
- Hold a sponsored fast and give the money to charity.

☐ *Conclusion*

Place a jug of dirty water (or a number of jugs spread around the church) where it can be seen, along with a small chunk of dry bread or a spoonful of rice.

Encourage everyone to be silent for a moment and to imagine what it might be like to go hungry – to have had no food for some time except for unclean water and a small amount of bread or rice.

 Use the prayer for creation and harvest from *Patterns for Worship* (Church House Publishing, 1989), p. 120.

12th SUNDAY AFTER PENTECOST

 The witnessing community

The Christian community is the witnessing community, and as such Christians need to re-examine their lives periodically to be sure that they are equipped to take God's message to the world.

Matthew 5.13–16

Note: Either at the start of the service or before the Gospel produce the mime described below.

Stand, candle, matches and cardboard tube.
Overhead projector or board and paper, and felt-tip pen.
Primed people to empty pockets and bags, if desired.
One or two black plastic rubbish bags.
Sugar-paper and Pritt-Tack.
Felt-tip pen.
Pictures or overhead projector transparencies for prayers, if desired.

☐ *Introduction: Mime*

At the start of the service, or before the Gospel, act out the words. 'No one lights a lamp to put it under a tub'.

In silence, one person brings in a candle, places it on a stand, steps back to admire the effect, lights the candle, and admires it again. Finally they produce a hollow tube of cardboard and place over the candle, which effectively hides the flame from sight. Completely satisfied they go out.

If this is carried out at the beginning of the service the appropriate words from the Gospel should be read out after the mime has taken place. Otherwise read the Gospel straight after the mime, with no introduction.

☐ *Comment*

Comment that today's Gospel reading (Matthew 5.13–16) says that Christians are like the salt of the earth, and again, like lights placed on a stand for all to see.

Note that Jesus asks what good we are if we lose our flavour, or if we are like a light that is covered up. The only good things about salt are that it can preserve food and add flavour to what we eat. Otherwise it has little use. Similarly with the candle or lamp. There is no point in lighting a candle and then covering it up so that no one can see the flame.

Jesus says our faith should infect other people, just like salt flavours food. He also says that our faith should shine like a light so that other people can see it and be attracted towards God's light. However, all too often the witnessing community has become like the candle that is placed on a stand and then hidden.

You might wish to ask the congregation to think of modern metaphors more appropriate to their lives than salt or light, since many people no longer use salt or candle light.

Put any suggestions up on an overhead projector or board. Example:

- the fruit in a fruit-cake
- the oil in a car
- the filling in a sandwich.

☐ *Activity: The handbag and pocket*

Offer to show the congregation what has happened to the witnessing community, by encouraging everyone to empty out their pockets and handbags. Alternatively use a primed group of people of all ages.

Ask them to identify the following:

- *Emergency items*: Plasters, aspirins, AA membership card, the number to ring when the windscreen breaks, etc.
- *Everyday items*: Money, pens, combs, etc.
- *Out-of-date items*: Old coupons, pens that don't work, last year's diary, old money, etc.
- *Items of sentimental value*: Letters, dried flowers, broken jewellery, pictures, etc.
- *Complete rubbish*: Sweet papers, soggy tissues, old receipts, etc. (Inform the congregation that all the rubbish will be collected up and disposed of at the end of this 'sermon'.)

Allow families to explore mother's handbag if permitted, and ask her to explain different items.

☐ *Comment*

After a few minutes gather the attention back and remind the congregation that Jesus said we are witnesses. As witnesses to the news of Jesus Christ we must be ready to act at any time. However, all too often we are not very effective witnesses because we have become like the contents of our pockets and handbags:

- *Full of unused emergency equipment.* Suggest that all too often our Bibles and prayer books are in pristine condition and never used. Even prayer, the regular communication channel with God, sometimes remains unused.
- *Possessing some everyday items.* Suggest that there is some good in all of us that we do use – love, kindness, generosity, for instance.
- *Cluttered with time-expired elements.* Suggest that all too often we are cluttered with time-expired elements. We make rash promises that we fail to keep. We never really plunge in and

try the Christian life. All too often we live on the fringe.

- *Cluttered with items of sentimental value.* Suggest that all too often we are held back by a sentimental attachment to the past. We cling to old ideas, old traditions, and the way we did things in the past. While not everything of the present is superior, our sentimental attachment to the past can keep us looking backwards and not forwards.
- *Cluttered with rubbish.* Suggest that we spend our time arguing about unimportant things. Use examples from your own situation, e.g. removal of pews, or whether toddlers should be in church for the whole service, etc.

☐ *Conclusion*

Finally gather up all the rubbish that has been turned out of bags and pockets and collect in a plastic sack. Simply comment that this, like the rubbish in our own lives, needs removing!

 For the confession this week concentrate on the theme of witnessing and our failure to carry out Jesus' commands as effectively as we might because of our weakness. Look at any failures, either locally or nationally, where Christian witness might have made a difference.

For the intercessions the use of pictures or over-head projector transparencies highlighting world issues concerning witnessing would be appropriate. Mention the spread of the church in Africa or the freeing of restrictions on the church in Russia.

13th SUNDAY AFTER PENTECOST

The suffering community

Christians should be helped to see that suffering is not necessarily negative. It can sometimes be the prelude to great joy: Jesus suffered on Good Friday but rose on Easter Sunday. Suffering has much to teach us about ourselves, about other people and about God.

Acts 20.17–35   Matthew 10.16–22

 Sufficient copies of the questions for each group.

> Paper, and paint or crayons if desired.
> Taped music, or a cd and player, as desired.

☐ *Introduction*

Comment that the theme for the day is 'the suffering community'. Add that we all know there is much suffering in this life, for our television screens and papers are filled with the stories of other people's suffering. However, it is a subject that we prefer to avoid if it gets too close to home.

Note that although the theme is actually the suffering of the *Christian* community, looking at suffering in general will help to think about the suffering of the church community.

☐ *Groupwork*

Create small groups of mixed ages to look at the following questions with regard to the theme of suffering. Don't exclude the children, even if you decide to opt for a separate group for the very youngest. Children are more likely to find this theme approachable than many adults!

- Ask every member of the group if they have suffered in their life. (For example because of the death of a loved one; through an injury; or because they were extremely unhappy.)
- What did each member of the group learn from their suffering?

Encourage people to be honest and share their feelings, but do not push them – some people may still be suffering! Help children to understand what is being said and enable them to speak of what they have suffered (separation from a parent, death of a grandparent or animal, when they first went to school, etc.).

The groups should be instructed to allow each person to speak without interrupting them at all.

Finally, request each group member to make *affirming* comments about people in the group and their experiences.

Examples of an affirming comment:

- 'I was very impressed with the way you coped with ...'
- 'Your faith seems to have grown because of the way you suffered!'
- 'Because of your experience you were able to help Mrs ...'

These comments should not be 'manufactured'. Where someone has obviously not grown through their suffering, but has actually regressed, it is enough that they can talk about the experience!

Optional work for young children

Young children might prefer to be in a group of their own. Discuss with them the times when they have been hurt. What happened to them? Was Mummy or Daddy always able to 'make it better'? (Or was the Doctor able to make it better?)

Ensure that they understand that God is always unhappy when we are hurt.

Can the children think of ways that they can help other children who are hurt to feel better? Perhaps they can make a card for someone who is ill, or go and visit them.

Optional work for adults

Some adults may prefer to work on their own if times of suffering are still too close to be examined. Encourage them to paint or draw a picture that represents their feeling at the time when their suffering was at its worst, and then to paint or draw a picture to represent how they feel now. Stress the use of colour and shape rather than actual representations.

☐ *Comment*

The New Testament reading (Acts 20.17–35) and the Gospel reading (Matthew 10.16–22) speak of the suffering that the newly founded Christian church is to undergo. There are no answers as to why we have to suffer. Jesus simply says that those of us who endure (keep going) will finally be saved. The Christian who learns more about their faith because of their suffering, and the Christian who because of their suffering is later able to help others, will one day be rewarded.

Perhaps the most important point about suffering is that it is the only time in our life when we are totally dependent on God. We stop trying to sort it out ourselves, and simply trust in God, for only God has the answers.

☐ *Conclusion*

Close this part of the service by playing a piece of music (on a tape or cd rather than the organ or piano) and allow the congregation to think quietly for a moment about all those who are suffering now.

Suitable music:

'Nimrod' (*Enigma Variations*) by Elgar
Symphony No 40 by Mozart
'Saturn' from *The Planets* by Holst

Note: If you are intending to use the service for the 15th Sunday after Pentecost you will need to organize a small group of adults and children to produce some short sketches.

14th SUNDAY AFTER PENTECOST

The family

The congregation are encouraged to experience what it is like to be a member of a different family, and to go on a search together.

Luke 11.1–13

> Copies of the Lord's Prayer.
> Sugar-paper.
> Paints, crayons or felt-tip pens.
> One or two dictionaries.
> Copies of the Caribbean Lord's Prayer

☐ *Introduction*

Prior to the service give each person as they enter church a number. These will become the means of dividing people up into new families. Aim for about six people in each family. For example, if you expect 60 people to be present, you will need to number slips of paper from one to ten, six times. Give out the numbers totally at random, so that those who enter church together will find themselves in different groups.

Place large-scale numbers around the church: e.g. put a number 1 at the back of the church, a number 2 in the choir, etc. This will help for quick dispersal when people are trying to find their new families.

☐ *Comment*

The theme for the service is 'the family'. Very often we take our families for granted, and it is only when we no longer have them that we appreciate them.

Families rarely have the chance to talk about what they do and why they do it. Comment, however, that you are going to give everyone a chance to overcome these faults today.

☐ *Activity: Create a family*

Remind the congregation that everyone received a number when they entered church (if they didn't, give some more out at this point) and explain that this was to help create totally new families. Invite them to find the members of their new family by going to the same large number which you have placed in church.

Point out that very small children might prefer to stay with parents or brothers or sisters, though do give them the choice.

Once everyone has found their number ask them to sit down with the members of their new family and give them a copy of the tasks below:

Tasks for the family

1. Introduce yourself to each member of your new family.

2. Decide what you would be like to be in your new family (e.g. aunt, father, sister – you can be anyone!).

3. Where does your family live? Can you create an imaginary place to live in? Do you have any pets? Are you rich, or poor?

4. Decide together what you think the most important and special thing is about your new family (this might be health, or the dog, or ???).

5. Make up a prayer for families, and say it. The prayer can be as formal or informal as you like.

Give each new family an activity that they must do *together*, from the list below. The activities should be allocated so that as many as possible are completed. You might need a dictionary on hand.

1. Read the Lord's Prayer. What do you think the words 'Our Father' mean? Together as a family decide what you think a father should be like. Draw a father and surround him with words or comments that describe him. Give the picture the title 'Our Father'.

2. Read the Lord's Prayer. What do you think the words 'in heaven' mean? Together as a family decide what you think heaven might be like. Use a piece of paper headed 'In heaven' and list all the things you come up with.

3. Read the Lord's Prayer. What do you think 'Hallowed be your name' means? Together as a family think about how special people's names are to them, and decide why you think God's name might be special. Create a picture using the following names for God: Jehovah, Yahweh, God, Lord, Father, Holy Spirit, Holy Ghost, Jesus, Christ. Give the picture the title 'Hallowed be your name'.

4. Read the Lord's Prayer. What do you think 'Your kingdom come' means? Together as a family think about kings and kingdoms. What do you think might be special about God's kingdom? Think of as many words as possible that might describe his kingdom and write them down on a sheet of paper. Give the work the title 'Your kingdom come'.

5. Read the Lord's Prayer. What do you think 'Your will be done' means? Together as a family think about how often we want our own way in life. What does it feel like when we don't get our own way, and how often do we really let other people have their own way? If God had his own way what would we be like? Create drawings of people getting their own way, and put a cross neatly through each drawing. Give the picture the title 'Your will be done'.

6. Read the Lord's Prayer. What do you think 'Give us today our daily bread' means? Together, as a family create a drawing about these words. Give the picture the title 'Give us today our daily bread'.

7. Read the Lord's Prayer. What do you think 'Forgive us our sins' means? Together as a family decide what sins you think you ought to ask God to forgive you for. Draw a picture of someone kneeling in prayer and surround them with words or pictures describing as many sins as the group can imagine. Give the picture the title 'Forgive us our sins'.

8. Read the Lord's Prayer. What do you think 'as we forgive those who sin against us' means? Together as a family talk about forgiving other people when they have hurt us. What kind of things do we have to forgive, and do we find this hard? Together write a prayer asking God to help you forgive other people. Give the prayer the title 'As we forgive those who sin against us'.

9. Read the Lord's Prayer. What do you think 'Lead us not into temptation' means? Together as a group discuss what tempts you. Draw a picture describing some of the things that tempt people. Give the picture the title 'Lead us not into temptation'.

10. Read the Lord's Prayer. What do you think 'but deliver us from evil' means? Together as a group discuss evil in our lives today. Create a prayer that starts 'But deliver us from evil' and list all the things that you feel are evil.

11. Read the Lord's Prayer. What do you think 'For the kingdom, the power and the glory are yours now and for ever' means? Together as a group discuss eternity. Create a drawing that shows the power and glory of God, and give it the title 'For the kingdom, the power, and the glory are yours now and for ever'.

12. Read the Lord's Prayer. What do you think 'Amen' means? Together as a group decide other words that might mean 'Amen'. Then create a poster with all the things that you are agreeing to in the Lord's Prayer. Put a large tick alongside them, and give the poster the title 'Amen'.

Note: Churches with small numbers might wish to edit the groupwork above, and pick out some of the sections of the Lord's Prayer.

□ *Conclusion*

Encourage all the families to stay together for the rest of the service (even the choir if possible), and have coffee or a meal together afterwards. You might want to discuss what this feels like at some other time.

Hold a plenary session to hear what happened from different families, or alternatively if the optional work was included encourage everyone to put up their work (in the correct order) and spend a few moments reading the completed assignment.

Sing the Caribbean Lord's Prayer (JP).

15th SUNDAY AFTER PENTECOST

Those in authority
It is important to understand how each one of us uses authority in order to pray for those 'in authority'.

1 Kings 3.4–15

> A mixed group of about six people (adults and children) of all ages, to carry out the demonstration sketches.
> Three placards with description of sketch on each.
> Person to hold up the placards.
> Overhead projector, or board and paper, and felt-tip pen.
> Artwork, if desired.

☐ *Introduction*
Comment that the theme for the service is 'Those in authority'. Remind the congregation that everyone present is someone 'in authority' – in other words, a leader!

As soon as we are old enough to make friends we find that there are times when what we want clashes with what others want. Often we get our own way, and friends give in to our 'authority'. Sometimes authority can be used in the wrong way.

Refer to the Old Testament reading (1 Kings 3.4–15), regarding the right use of authority and power. When Solomon was made king he asked God for help with governing his country. God was so pleased that he had not asked for great wealth or long life, that he decided to make Solomon very wise. He also made him rich since he had not requested this.

Comment that it is important that we learn how to use leadership skills in the right way, and for the right reasons. There are a number of ways to use authority, and sometimes we use them in the wrong way with those we love and with whom we work.

☐ *Sketches: Leadership styles*
Prior to this service organize a small group of adults and children to produce some short sketches to demonstrate a variety of leadership styles.

Ensure that the actors know the story-lines for the different scenes before the service. The sketches, however, are all ad-libbed. A placard should be held up as each sketch is shown, indicating the style of leadership: authoritarian, permissive, or democratic.

AUTHORITARIAN

A parent *directs* other members of the family to do various jobs.
For example: 'Ben, take that upstairs for me!' 'Sue, put a
cardigan on – now!' An automatic response by the rest of the
family is expected and little if any comment will be needed
from them. Any argument will receive automatic censure by
the parent who is always in the right!

PERMISSIVE

An older teenager is in charge of a group of younger children.
He or she allows the group to make all the decisions. The
children could be trying to decide what to do for the afternoon.
Ensure that inappropriate choices are made by the children
(and acquiesced in by the teenager), perhaps about what film
to see. The permissive style of leadership allows *anything* to
happen!

DEMOCRATIC

This is a discussion group with three or four adults and
children. All opinions are held to be valued and are listened to
accordingly. Although someone is obviously in charge the
decision is taken by the whole group and the leader does not
give up all their authority, but is a first among his or her peers.
Occasionally they may need to exert some authority. For
example: 'I think it's about time we took a vote on this!' The
subject discussed could be 'What charity should we raise money
for this year?' There should be some disagreement, so that the
group will have to work at getting a unanimous agreement.

☐ *Discussion*

Point out to the congregation that the illustrations only give
examples of three leadership styles: authoritarian, permissive, and
democratic. There are others!

Write the names of the leadership styles up on an over-head
projector or board, and continue by discussing with the
congregation situations where each of these could best be used.

Ask for suggestions as to which leadership style would be best in
the following situations:

- at a fire
- on deciding about the family holiday
- when faced with people who are gossiping
- at a PCC meeting on the subject of the summer fete
- when walking with children near a cliff edge
- when discussing what children should do with their pocket
  money

Optional | If your congregation possesses an artist you may wish to present the above suggestions in picture form.

Optional
role-play | Set up a number of groups and give them all a scenario for a piece of role-play. The situation should be somewhat fraught.

Appoint one member of the group as the leader and inform them that they are to try and defuse the situation using an appropriate leadership style.

Appoint another member of the group to be an observer. They are to report back to the group at the end with their observations on the effect of the leadership *style* used (not, it must be noted, on the particular leader), and its effect on the group.

Situations suitable:

- A family argument over a daughter staying out too late at night.
- A group of children who cannot decide what game to play.
- An argument in the choir over which hymn tune to use.
- A family in a car who are undecided about which road to take to get to their destination.

☐ *Conclusion*

Comment that leadership is often a matter of being humble and allowing others to take the lead. Leaders should not always be permissive for this can sometimes be dangerous.

Jesus knew when to be authoritarian, as when throwing the traders out of the temple or commanding evil spirits to leave people, *and* he knew when to be humble when washing his disciples' feet or, supremely, when submitting to death.

Comment that all of us in our own way are 'in authority', and when measured against Jesus we can see that as leaders we have much to learn.

Invite a number of people to come forward and light small candles while saying short one-line prayers for those in authority:

- the Queen and members of the royal family;
- the Prime Minister and members of the cabinet;
- members of parliament;
- local MPs;
- the local mayor;
- town or parochial council;
- vicar or minister, and church governing body.

The response by the congregation could be:

'Lord, give them wisdom.'

16th SUNDAY AFTER PENTECOST

The neighbour
Love is at the heart of the Christian message – love of God and of our neighbour.

1 John 4.15–end   Luke 16.19–end

Overhead projector or board and paper, and felt-tip pens.
Five adults and four children to act as neighbours.
Group A: Information for review of neighbourhood scheme, or to start preparing a new scheme.
Maps and information on locality to initiate prayer plan. Paper and pen.
Group B: Yellow pages phone book and maps of locality. Paper and pen.
Group C: Christian Aid or Oxfam information and posters. Information on church projects. Video and video machine. World map and information on countries. CMS banana trading game. Information on One World Week. Paper and pen.

☐ *Introduction: Buzz session*

Ask the congregation to turn to their neighbour and talk about 'friends'. What makes a good friend? How long do they keep their friends? Who are their friends? How have friends helped them?

After a few minutes ask for comments from adults and children. Concentrate on the differences between their answers. Children might feel friends are more transitory and that allegiances change, or that friends let you down. Adults who made friends years ago may want to disagree with some of these statements.

If possible, come up with some characteristics of a good friend, and put these up on an overhead projector or board.

Example:

Characteristics of a good friend
– trustworthy
– fun
– reliable
– have things in common
– different (or similar) characters

☐ *Comment*

Jesus said we are to love our neighbour as ourselves, but while it can be easy to love our friend and to do anything we can for them, it is sometimes not so easy to love our neighbour. A neighbour may or may not be a friend!

Refer to the Gospel reading (Luke 16.19–end) and the inability of the rich man to see Lazarus at his gate.

☐ *Demonstration: Who is our neighbour?*

Prior to the service prime some adults and children to be a variety of characters. If desired they could dress up in suitable clothing. They will each need a copy of the script below.

The characters should come out to the front of the church and announce loudly who they are to the congregation. Ensure that microphones are used if possible, and that younger children are confident of their parts. Organize the numbers involved to suit your church and your own circumstances.

1st adult: I am Benjamin and I live in London.
2nd adult: I am Mary and I live in London next door to Benjamin.
1st child: I am David and I live with my Mum and Dad two doors away from Benjamin – in London.

2nd child:	I am Sarah and I live in a house at the bottom of the garden – in London, near Benjamin.
3rd adult:	I am Christine and I live in the same road as Benjamin – in London.
3rd child:	I am Jane and I live in London – the same town as Benjamin.
4th adult:	I am Amal and I live in Essex – the same county as Benjamin.
4th child:	I am Howard and I live in England – the same country as Benjamin.
5th adult:	I am Feodor and I live in India – the same world as Benjamin.

Ask the question, 'Who is Benjamin's neighbour?' and allow the congregation (particularly the children) to decide for themselves that they are all Benjamin's neighbours.

☐ *Groupwork: Loving one's neighbours*
Create a number of groups to look at projects designed to help our neighbour:

GROUP A: NEIGHBOURHOOD SCHEMES
Review any neighbourhood scheme in operation and see if it can be improved, perhaps to involve children and teenagers in the day-to-day work.

Alternatively, begin to plan a neighbourhood scheme, which may involve appointing street wardens to pass on information about the sick or those who require help or prayers. Again build in a place for all ages in this scheme – children to octogenarians.

Or create a prayer plan to pray for all the different areas in your parish or area. You might wish to include farms, shops, or offices and those who work in them, as well as residential areas.

GROUP B: PEOPLE WHO NEED HELP LOCALLY
Draw up a list of local organizations or people who may need your help. These might include homeless hostels, Samaritans, charity shops, Headway, hospices, hospitals, schools for the blind or deaf, prisons, etc.

Or organize people to contact these groups to find out what, if any, help they might need. Resolve to begin organizing the church community to help them.

Or initiate stamp, card, paper or can collecting to raise money for charities.

Or allow the children in the group to come up with some way in which they can help in the near future: for instance, by collecting clothes or items for charity shops; holding a mile of

5p coins; or by collecting newspapers or cans. The adults of the group should then resolve to support the children in their efforts, and ensure that their ideas happen and the proceeds go to charity.

GROUP C: PEOPLE WHO NEED HELP ABROAD
Prior to the service contact Christian Aid or Oxfam for information regarding overseas projects. Display these for others in the church to see.

Alternatively, update yourselves on projects the church may be involved in already, or initiate a new project concerned with overseas humanitarian work.

Or watch a video about overseas aid.

Or prepare a list of food items that you would prefer Christians not to buy from the supermarket because of their association with corrupt governments.

Or play the CMS banana trading game, available from CMS.

Or resolve to observe One World Week in October and start to prepare for this.

☐ *Conclusion*
Come back together and briefly share your experiences.

 Concentrate the intercessions on humanitarian issues both at home and abroad.

Note: If you intend using the service for the 18th Sunday after Pentecost you will need to organize the collection of photographs.

17th Sunday after Pentecost

 The proof of faith
The way that we live our lives as Christians is evidence or proof of our faith in God. This is explored through a dramatized story.

Galatians 2.15–3.9   Luke 7.1–10

A story-teller and script.
Adults and children to act the parts of:

- the King
- Mother Ginger
- sports team and coach
- army and General.

Suitable hats for all the cast.
A chair, a fruit pie, binoculars, soft ball, and crown.

☐ *Introduction*

Tell the following story with the help of some suitably primed
adults and children.

You will probably need to practise the story at least once with
the cast, but they could run through their actions just prior to the
service. The actors do not mime everything, but merely give an
indication of some of the action. The reader should hold the
attention of the congregation at other times.

Try to ensure a mix of adults and children among the actors,
and rely upon hats for costumes. These could be made out of
cardboard if necessary. The King should be fairly
unprepossessing!

You will need one chair at a central point.

Optional | The story could be told without actions if desired, or with the
reader wearing different hats as appropriate.

☐ *Story: King Proof*

Once upon a time
there was a land called
Proof. Now Proof was
only a small kingdom.
Indeed King Proof
knew all the people in
his kingdom, and on
sunny summer days
would drop in to see
his subjects.

(Enter a King. He walks down the church, through or past the
congregation, and sits down on a chair.)

He liked nothing better than to call and see old Mother Ginger,
and doze under her apple tree in the warm air while she made
him some fruit tartlets.

(Enter Mother Ginger carrying a plate with one tart on it.
Gives the King the tart, who eats it.)

One day as he waited for the warm tarts it occurred to him to
wonder why there were never apple tarts. He preferred apple tarts
to jam tarts. Perhaps it was because the apple trees had no fruit
he thought, as he gazed up at the branches of the apple tree.
Come to think of it, the apple trees never seemed to have any
apples on them.

Still, the proof of the pudding was in the eating, he thought, as
he finally bit into the warm jam tart.

The first bite almost made him fall off the bench. The tart was
dreadful. In fact it wasn't just dreadful ... it was ... well, words
almost failed him ... it was AWFUL!

(King jumps up, and shouts '*The proof of the pudding is in the
eating.*' King storms off, followed by very unhappy looking
Mother Ginger.)

King Proof was fed up, nothing seemed to be going right. It was
only two days to the national games, and he so wanted his
favourite sports team to win.

The coach had assured him that the team were all fit and
healthy, and on the day would undoubtedly win the race.
Certainly they looked in good condition. But the coach had said
the same the previous year, and the Proof team had still come
last.

(King Proof enters and walks to centre. He could be carrying a
pair of binoculars.)

The King made his way to the sports ground to watch the
team's last training session.

(Enter a number of adults and children, who 'hop-scotch'
down the aisle towards the King. None of the group can
actually hop-scotch, and frequently go off balance and fall
over.)

Here was his pride and joy, the hop-scotch team. Look how
they went down the course. The King drew himself up proudly,
ready to greet the coach and his team. Perhaps, the King thought,
he ought to give them a last-minute pep-talk.

(At this point the King raises his binoculars before the team get
to him, and he sees them for the first time.)

But surely this was not *HIS* team, this raggle-taggle bunch of ...!
'Odd-balls' was really the only word for them, he thought. The
glasses almost fell from his hands. This wasn't dreadful ... this
was ... AWFUL!

(King jumps up and down in anger, and shouts '*The proof of the running is in the race.*' The King storms off, followed by a rather weary looking team.)

By the afternoon King Proof had cheered up again. He was never fed-up for very long, and anyway he had remembered that his army were on manoeuvres in a wood just below his castle.

Perhaps he would go and see them. The General would be sure to be pleased that he'd taken an interest in them, particularly as some new recruits had joined recently.

(The King enters at the back and takes off his crown, and puts on an army hat.)

Taking off his crown, which he really only wore when he was King and not the Commander of the army, he put on his Commander's hat. It did look rather nice, he thought.

Feeling pleased with himself the King strolled through the gardens and down into the woods below the castle.

(King moves down towards the front of the congregation.)

It was quiet in the woods, and the King found himself tiptoeing, almost afraid to make a noise. Where was the army? He couldn't hear them. Usually they were very noisy with their guns and cannons.

(Enter a number of adults and children dressed in a motley selection of army clothing from the back of the church. They play a game with a soft ball, moving down the aisle towards the King.)

Something made the King turn round, some noise or movement, and he paused leaning against a tree, hardly able to believe his eyes. For there in the clearing behind him were the members of his army ... words almost failed him ... playing with a ball!

(The General approaches the King and salutes.)

'Hello, sir!' The voice made the King jump. Before him was his General, a neat salute accomplished. 'I'm afraid you've come at a bad time, sir. They've gone on strike, you see. They're not prepared to fight any more!'

King Proof swelled with anger ... he spluttered ... he went purple. 'It's a disgrace', he finally said. 'It's ... dreadful ... No! It's ... AWFUL!'

(The King jumps up and down in anger and shouts '*The proof of the army is in the fighting*!' The King storms off, followed slowly by a dejected army.)

By the next morning King Proof had made a decision. Things couldn't go on like this, the kingdom of Proof would be a laughing stock. He would have to do something to make sure that things improved.

(Enter King, deep in thought, to seat.)

The question was, what could he do? Perhaps he could give everyone in the kingdom a pep-talk and remind them of their duties to him, the King.

This seemed like a good idea, so finally he called for his royal messenger, who came at a run.

(Enter the royal messenger, running backwards.)

Well, amended the King, it was more of a stumble than a run. However, he pretended not to notice and gave the messenger the royal proclamation.

(King gives the messenger a scroll of paper. Messenger exits.)

Shortly the people of the kingdom began to gather before the King.

(All the cast enter one at a time.)

What on earth could he want? They have never been summoned like this before. What was the matter?

The King stood up and looked at his people, the frown upon his face even more noticeable. What a rabble they looked, he thought. Really they were not fit to be citizens of Proof and *his* people. It was quite ... AWFUL!

(King stands and shouts, *The Proof of the pudding is in the eating!*')

Now, the people were quite used to their King shouting such sayings at them, and they understood this particular one very well. It was no good saying your cake was delicious, if when it was tasted it was awful! And it was no good saying you were a good sports team, if you couldn't even run a race! And it was no good saying you were an army if you couldn't even fight!

But the people of Proof were also fed up with their King, and so this time they turned their backs upon him, and they shouted:

(Everyone turns towards the congregation and shouts together, '*The proof of the King is in the kingdom!*' With that they all go out chanting, '*The proof of the pudding is in the eating! The proof of the King is in the kingdom!*' The King bows his head and remains quite still. As the chants continue the rest of the cast begin to exit. When they reach the door(s) they turn to face the congregation, and shout, '*The proof of faith is in ...*' Each

member of the cast should have been given one word to shout.
Their words should come one after the other. However, it will
not matter if two shout together, or there is a gap. Use words
like:

action	giving	sharing
good works	helping others	helping
loving others	listening	doing
	caring	

These final words can be directed by the story-teller in the
manner of a musical director conducting a choir. Finally after a
pause the King and the story-teller should exit.)

□ *Conclusion*
Simply state that faith in God must show itself in the way that we
live, or 'The proof of faith is in good works.'

18th SUNDAY AFTER PENTECOST

The offering of life
As Christians we should be growing spiritually, just as we grow
physically. We are reminded therefore that we should not leave
our Christian gifts unused. They should be in constant use.

Matthew 25.14–30

Display of baby photographs, numbered.
Pencils and paper.
Questions for discussion put up on an overhead projector or
   board.
'Floating leaders', if desired, to help with discussion.

□ *Introduction: Activity*
In the weeks before this service gather together as many baby
photographs from members of the congregation as possible. Make
sure that all are numbered and marked on a check list. The
photographs should be mounted and hung round the walls of the
church.
   Give each member of the congregation a pencil and paper, and

invite them to come and examine the photographs to see if they can guess the identity of the babies.

Encourage them to look at the colour of eyes and hair, and the shape of nose and mouth. Then compare these to the people present. When they feel they know the identity of the babies, they should make a note of the name.

When everyone is seated again ask for suggestions as to the identity of each baby before revealing the truth.

☐ *Discussion*

Discuss whether it was easy to guess the identity of the babies. How many had changed completely? What if any, characteristics had stayed the same?

☐ *Comment*

Remind the congregation that just as our outer appearance changes from the time we are born, so do other things. We should also be growing and changing as Christians. This change should be just as dramatic as the physical one that is taking place.

Many of the congregation will have been baptized as babies or young adults. For some this was a long while ago. Just as they have changed out of all recognition physically so they should have changed spiritually.

Comment that each of us have been given gifts which can be of use in our Christian life. The Gospel reading (Matthew 25.14–30), reminds us that it is no good burying these gifts so that no growth takes place. Rather we should be making use of our gifts so that they have a chance of growing with us.

☐ *Buzz groups*

Encourage everyone to turn to their neighbour and discuss:

- What gifts did God give them (e.g. what are they good at?)
- How have they used these gifts throughout their life?
- Have they grown spiritually since their baptism or confirmation, or perhaps this year?

If possible each person's analysis should be confirmed or denied by their neighbour.

The questions could be put up on an over-head projector or board for all to see. Allow at least five minutes for discussion and use one or two 'floating leaders' if necessary to keep the talk going if it starts to flag. Also ensure that all children have an adult to talk to, and that the discussion is truly two-way discussion.

☐ *Conclusion: Renewal of baptismal vows*

Conclude this part of the service by inviting all the congregation to renew their baptism vows, as a reminder of our need to keep growing spiritually in the same way as we have grown and changed physically. The words for the renewal of baptismal vows can be found on page 276 of the Alternative Service Book.

19th SUNDAY AFTER PENTECOST

The life of faith
Faith is what the Christian lives by, even when they may feel that there is little hope for the future. Faith can overcome fear.

Daniel 6.10–23

> Overhead projector or board and paper, and felt-tip pen.
> Group leaders as required.
> Tape recorder(s) and music for Groups A, D and E.
> Paper and pen.
> Children's story book.
> Paper and paint, or coloured pencils.
> Alternative Service Book.

☐ *Introduction: Buzz group*
Ask the congregation to own up to what really scares them. Everyone will probably have their own private fear, no matter how old or how strong they are. Encourage them to turn to a neighbour and speak for a few moments about the things that really scare them and any particular incident that comes to mind.

☐ *Discussion: Our fears*
Make a list on an overhead projector or board of the things that people really fear. These might be:

fire	snakes
darkness	lifts
moths	open spaces
heights	being shut in

daddy-long-legs	being attacked
spiders	hospital
dentist	being made fun of

Ask if anyone has managed to overcome their fear of anything and listen to one or two speakers' experiences.

Comment that often our worry over the fear causes us more problems than the actual thing itself. Ask people how many times, for instance, they have been in a fire, or been bitten by a snake, or fallen from a great height. Some of us have never been hurt, and our fear seems to be caused by knowing that we could be hurt. At other times the fear is out of all proportion – as with fear of spiders, moths or ants.

☐ *Groupwork*
Divide the congregation into groups to continue looking at this theme.

GROUP A: OVERCOMING OUR FEARS
Under an experienced leader establish one or more groups that enable people to continue looking at their fears. Encourage them to talk about their fears, and to suggest ways that they might deal with them one step at a time.

Ensure that no one makes facile judgements on fears that are probably very deep. Do not make the obvious judgement that to fear means we have little faith. However, do remind the group that God loves and cares for us every moment of our day and night.

If possible end the session by listening to some peaceful music. Any of the following would be suitable:

'First Song' by Ralph McTell
Symphony No 9 from *New World* (2nd movement) by
    Dvorak
'Air' from Suite No 3 in D by Bach
Piano Concerto No 5 (2nd movement) by Beethoven
Venus Suite from *The Planets* by Holst.

Alternatively spend some time in prayer, concentrating on specific fears. Encourage the group to keep in contact with one another, and to continue listening to each other.

GROUP B: STORYTIME
Create one or more small groups to make up stories about people overcoming their fears. Each group should collectively write one children's story designed to help children

with their fears. A variety of subjects could be dealt with: spiders; being away from Mum or Dad; fire; etc. The group will need a scribe who has paper and a pen, and will be prepared to complete the story afterwards if necessary.

Arrange for the stories to be collated and printed for sale to the congregation at a later date.

GROUP C: YOUNG CHILDREN'S GROUP

Invite a story-teller to read one of the following to a group of young children.

The Owl Who Was Afraid of the Dark by Jill Tomlinson (Methuen 1992).

A Book of Ghosts, illustrated by Pam Adams and Ceri Jones (Child's Play 1984).

Note: The second book is about a child who is afraid of 'ghosts' – all of which turn out to be ordinary household objects.

GROUP D: FEAR PICTURES

If you have a separate room from that used by Group A play any of the following pieces of music, and then ask this group to draw or paint a picture based on what they hear.

Finale from *Don Giovanni* by Mozart
'Symphonie Fantastique' by Berlioz
Parts of *Rite of Spring* by Stravinsky
The Planets by Holst
Carmina Burana by Orff

GROUP E: MOVEMENT OR DANCE

Create a group to explore images of fear in movement or dance. This could be based on the music played for Group D.

☐ Conclusion

Hold a short plenary session to hear from each group, although the efforts of Group D and E could be seen later in the service if desired. Be careful not to demand a response from Group A, unless they feel this is appropriate.

Comment that the time when we are most fearful is the time to fall back on our faith. For faith doesn't require reason – it is more like a gut reaction! In our Old Testament reading (Daniel 6.10–23) we see Daniel thrown into the lions' den, yet despite what surely must have been terrrible fear, his faith triumphs. We are told that 'he trusted in his God'.

Use the collect for peace from the service for Morning Prayer in

the ASB (page 59), and the third collect from the service of
Evening Prayer in the ASB (page 70). You might feel the need to
change the word 'night' to read 'day' in the latter prayer.

20th SUNDAY AFTER PENTECOST

Endurance
St Paul says Christians are like athletes – continually in training
and aiming for the finishing line. His image conjures up a keen
forward-moving band of people. But how does this compare with
Christians today?

1 Corinthians 9.19–end   Matthew 7.13–27

> Children and adults wearing sports clothing.
> Keep-fit or aerobics expert, if desired.
> Paper, pencils and paint.
> Overhead projector or board and paper, and felt-tip pen.

☐ *Introduction*
Discuss with the congregation how many of them would consider
themselves sportsmen or -women (or -children).

If there is little response to this question ask how many people
play football, tennis, cricket, hockey, or golf. Use an over-head
projector or board to write up the different sports, and put a tick
for each sport in which there are participants. Include swimming,
walking and aerobics in the list so that older and younger
generations will be included.

Sports we take part in

Football	Swimming
Tennis	Walking
Cricket	Aerobics
Hockey	Horse riding
Golf	Cycling

Continue by discussing with the congregation what helps athletes to win or keep going when others have dropped out. These might include regular training, strength, stamina, a good eye for the ball, or the right food.

If appropriate, refer to any recent local or national game. Who won and why did they win?

☐ *Activity: Keeping fit*

Suggest that it is time that everyone started training in order to win or improve their game. If appropriate invite a local keep-fit or aerobics expert to help at this point.

If desirable arrange for a number of children and adults to come to church dressed in sports or jogging clothes. They can come out and help lead the congregation in the keep-fit exercises. Encourage the rest of the congregation to find a space in the church where they can carry out the exercises. Allow those who wish, to stay seated.

The expert should preferably start with simple warm-up exercises, and members of the congregation who have decided to stay seated should be encouraged to do suitable 'armchair' exercises, designed to loosen tight neck and shoulder muscles.

After some moments stop the exercises and allow everyone to resume their seats and regain their breath.

☐ *Comment*

Comment that the race they are really running is not a physical one, but a Christian race. In the New Testament reading (1 Corinthians 9.19–end), St Paul says that he runs straight for the finishing line and that he hardens his body and does not waste his punches. All his efforts and energies are put into reaching the finishing line.

In the Gospel reading (Matthew 7.13–27), Jesus says that our way will be hard, but we must still keep on trying.

Add that if we need to train to play sports, and to be an athlete, we also need to train to run the Christian race.

☐ *Groupwork*

Encourage the members of the congregation to join a group and continue working on the theme of Christian training.

GROUP A: CHRISTIAN TRAINING PROGRAMMES

As a group create a daily training programme for a Christian. Discuss how Christians become fit so that they can endure to the end if the race is gruelling. Keep the programme achievable, but build in optional extras for those who can do more. As with a diet or any training programme try to build in rewards.

If there is time, write this up on a large sheet of paper, and decorate with pictures of people getting fit. Head the work 'Our Christian training programme'. Put up for all to see.

GROUP B: OBSTACLES FOR THE CHRISTIAN ATHLETE

As a group discuss the difficulties that Christians might expect to meet on the Christian race-track. Examine the problems for different age groups, and make a list of them, together with any remedies that come to mind. For example, teenagers might experience peer pressure not to attend church.

Write the difficulties and any solutions up on paper and put up for all to see.

GROUP C: THE CHRISTIAN GOAL

As a group discuss what *is* the Christian goal – where are they running? Try to help the group make sense of heaven.

Then as a group draw or paint your ideas. These should be put up for all to see and photocopied if suitable for inclusion in the church magazine.

☐ *Conclusion*

Finally, encourage all the groups to put up their work even if they are not quite finished. Allow everyone a few moments to look at the different efforts.

Close with a prayer that 'we may see the need for training, and keep our eye on the goal ahead'.

Note: If you intend to use the service for the 21st Sunday after Pentecost, you will need to organize a 'time-share salesman'.

21st SUNDAY AFTER PENTECOST

The Christian hope

The Christian's hope is of eternal life sharing God's glory – surely the most perfect future we can conceive.

John 11.17–27

> Time-share salesman and 'sales-pitch'.
> Brochures, leaflets, or diagrams outlining the time-share.
> Paper and pencils, if desired.
> Frieze paper and paints or crayons, if desired.

☐ *Introduction*
Comment that you have agreed to allow someone to speak to the congregation this week because their message seems to be quite important.

Invite your 'speaker' forward, and then sit down.

☐ *Talk: The time-share scheme*
In the previous week arrange for someone to come and give a talk on a 'time-share scheme'. The speaker should create the most fabulous time-share scheme, perhaps somewhere in the Mediterranean.

Give it an interesting name and aim to produce a very slick talk as near as possible to a real time-share sales-pitch. It would help if overhead projector slides, diagrams or pictures could be shown, and if possible duplicated advertisements of the bogus time-share scheme given out. Of course, no price should be mentioned!

The speaker should talk heavily about 'an opportunity of a lifetime', 'only the discerning will really appreciate this custom-built enhanced investment', and 'suitability of tenure for those who are young or old'.

Finally, offer the listeners a challenge. If they can create a more attractive place than the idyllic holiday scheme, then the vicar/minister will award them a free place for life in . . . (name of the time-share scheme) for just a few formalities!

☐ *Activity: Plan a dream holiday*
Thank your speaker and then gather the congregation in small groups, or allow people to work on their own, as they please.

Ask them to create 'a holiday of a lifetime' that will suit their every need, ignoring the cost.

When most of the schemes are finished select some and share them with the rest of the congregation, pointing out all the merits of each holiday.

Optional | The holiday of a lifetime could be created by all the congregation together, using an overhead projector or board. In this case put *everything* into the holiday. It may be at the seaside, in the mountains, hot and temperate, etc., all at the same time.

□ *Comment*

Finally, offer your marvellous time-share scheme to everyone present; all they have to do is to complete a few formalities. Comment that everyone has deserved a place in your idyllic scheme, for life.

Refer to the formalities:

- Belief in God.
- Belief in his Son, Jesus Christ.
- Ask for forgiveness of sins (i.e. 'saying sorry').
- Try to carry out the commands of Jesus.

Admit that the fabulous time-share offer was in fact a way of describing the fabulous offer that Jesus Christ makes to us. He offers us eternal life, freedom from all the sins that we have committed, and a life with God in perfect bliss. Put in everyday terms, he offers us 'the holiday of a lifetime, all the time'.

Add that this is no forlorn hope, for the promise comes from the man who raised Lazarus to life four days after he had been put in the tomb. Martha says of Jesus, 'Even now I know that whatever you ask of God, God will grant you.'

It is this Jesus who offers us 'the holiday of a lifetime', with no strings. A holiday in the perpetual presence of a loving heavenly Father.

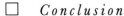 1. Young children may wish to create a frieze of things that they like to do on holiday. Older children or adults might like to add some words to the frieze. Simply explain that being with God is like going on holiday all the time.

2. As well as creating dream holidays, some of the congregation might like to create a 'Hope is . . .' chart. This could be displayed after or during the service, or used as the basis for intercessions.

□ *Conclusion*

 Close with a reminder of the Christian hope, possibly using the words from Romans 5.2, 5:

> We rejoice in our hope of sharing the glory of God . . . and hope does not disappoint us, because God's love has been poured into our hearts through the Holy Spirit.

Note: If you intend using the service for the Last Sunday after Pentecost, you will need to organize a group of people to create a sketch.

22nd SUNDAY AFTER PENTECOST

The two ways
We can choose to go God's way or our own way in life. The choice is ours.

Deuteronomy 11.18–28

Highway code signs, either put onto overhead projector transparencies or drawn large and attached to card. Overhead projector, if desired.

☐ *Introduction*
Tell the following story using highway code signs and allowing the congregation to call out the answers as they occur. Change the town and road names as appropriate to your own circumstances and elaborate as desired. It might be preferable if the story-teller is not yourself.

☐ *Story: The journey*
Last week I was travelling home from Bristol to Worcester on the M5. The traffic was very heavy. Everyone seemed to be overtaking, and generally behaving in quite a mad way.

Suddenly there was a flashing sign telling me to slow down to:

Slowly we all obeyed, the cars piling up behind one another.

Then a:

sign appeared.

Well you can imagine how we all groaned. I began to get anxious, as I had to be back home for a meeting at 8 o'clock, and it was by now 7.30 p.m.

On we crawled, stopping and starting. All we managed was a few yards each time. The signs were getting worse and worse, until finally this one appeared:

By now I'd given up all hope of ever getting home on time, when suddenly I noticed that we had almost reached the next junction – the one before my actual turning off – and this had been put up:

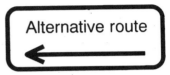

There was only a moment to decide. Did I take the other route, or did I stay where I was? At least I knew where the road went if I stayed where I was, and the fast lane *was* moving, even if very slowly. There was no one else taking the other route. Perhaps I'd better stay where I was!

On the other hand it said: so it must take me where I wanted to go. It couldn't be any worse than the motorway!

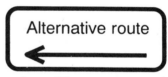

Finally I made the decision in the nick of time, and took the exit.

Wherever it went I followed! At every:

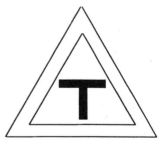

It never let me down – it was always there. When I got to a:

it was always there, leading me onwards towards home. All I had to do was to follow!

Indeed, I reached home with time to spare, and made my meeting easily.

(Tell the rest of this fast, encouraging the congregation to make their answers quickly.)

The story reminds us of today's theme.

Today we must:

STOP

We are faced with an:

Alternative route
←

We can choose to go God's way where he leads us, or we can stay in the traffic jam on the motorway.

Which route will you follow today?

☐ *Comment*
Briefly comment that the story reminds us we have a choice of which way to go in this life. We can follow God's way or our own way. In the Old Testament reading (Deuteronomy 11.18-28) Moses reminds the children of Israel that they can choose to follow God or go their own way. He promises God's protection and a blessing if they follow the way that he wants them to go, but if they choose to ignore God then he will curse them.

Refer to the fact that this is not a once-and-for-all choice, but a daily choice. Each time we are faced with temptation the choice is ours. Shall we take the difficult path and try to follow God's commandments, or shall we take the easy path which leads to separation from God? The choice is ours!

☐ *Groupwork*
Create small groups of mixed ages. Each group should have no more than six people in it if possible.

Ask the groups to create stories titled 'God's way' or 'Ignoring God's way', by telling the story 'in the round'. The group will need to decide before they start which title they are going to use.

One person should then start a story-line, for example:

1. 'Mary was late for school . . .'; or
2. 'John forgot the tomatoes that day . . .'

The next person then takes up the story and adds another sentence, for example:

1. 'She knew that she would be in trouble when her form teacher saw her'; or
2. 'What on earth was he going to say to his wife . . .'

As the story continues round the group, so each person adds another sentence, co-operating together to create a perfectly credible story. You are not aiming to produce a funny story-line, but simply to write a sensible story between you.

It might be helpful to remind the groups of the kind of elements they will need in their story. This could be written up on a board or overhead projector:

- some kind of problem in their story
- the hero or heroine is unsure what to do
- they have to make a decision
- what finally happens

☐ *Conclusion*

If there is time some of the groups might like to tell their completed story to the wider congregation. Alternatively these could be written up into a book of stories.

Hold up two signs (alternative route sign and a cross), and comment that today the congregation are faced with an alternative route that follows the cross. It will not be an easy route, but the end goal will be well worth the risk.

LAST SUNDAY AFTER PENTECOST

Citizens of heaven

We must live in a state of readiness in this life for we never know when our Lord will return for us.

Matthew 25.1–13

> Twelve adults and children prepared to offer a sketch.
> Various props for the sketch: sleeping bags, blankets, food, thermos flasks, etc.
> One of the twelve dressed as a famous person.

☐ *Introduction: Sketch*

Create a sketch with the help of twelve adults and children (or less if desired) to depict the story of the five wise and five foolish girls. The actors will need to have the story-line at least a week beforehand, but words should be ad-libbed as desired. If a rehearsal is necessary, meet just before the service. Ensure that words can be heard.

STORY-LINE

A famous person (football, pop, or royal) is due to come to your town the next day. Everyone is very excited and nothing else has been talked about for weeks in the town. Adults and children are all keen to see this person.

A group of people (perhaps members of a club, or a choir) decide to steal a march on everyone else by sleeping overnight on the pavement outside his (or her) hotel, in the hope of catching them as they arrive the evening before, or possibly the next morning as they leave for a variety of appointments in the town.

The ten adults and children meet outside the hotel. Half the group have planned their stay well and brought sleeping bags, extra jumpers or blankets, thermos flasks and food, and of course their autograph books. The other half of the group have just come as they are, with no food or sleeping bags, and of course no autograph books.

Late that night the group who are unprepared decide to go away to a hot dog stand to get some food and drink, and to see if they can get something for the star to autograph. Just after they have departed the famous person arrives, and is so impressed that the fans are prepared to sleep out in the cold all night just to see him/her, that he/she invites them into the hotel for an interview and a meal.

A few seconds later, after they have left, the second group of fans returns from the hot dog stand (which was closed) to be greeted with the news (perhaps by a doorman or the manager) that they have missed their idol, and that the other group were invited inside. The final words by the doorman or manager are 'You should have been prepared, for you never knew when he/she might come!' The group goes off dejectedly.

☐ *Comment*

The sketch you have just seen is a modern version of the story of the five sensible and the five foolish girls in the Gospel reading (Matthew 25.1–13).

Five of the girls were ready and organized and five were unprepared and missed the great event.

Add that Jesus was telling us to be prepared because we never know when he will return, and we must always be ready for him. That means we must live each moment as though he were about to return.

☐   *Buzz groups*

Ask the congregation to turn to their neighbour for a moment and talk about what three things they would like to do now if they knew that the Queen were to visit them tomorrow.

Possible things might be:

- clean the house
- buy some new clothes
- buy the Queen some flowers.

After a moment or two ask for some suggestions from different people. What differences are there between the ages, if any?

Then ask everyone to turn to their neighbour again and this time discuss what three things they would like to do now if they knew that Jesus was to return tomorrow.

After a moment or two ask for some suggestions – allowing people to answer or keep silent as they wish.

☐   *Conclusion*

Close with the words said to the five unprepared fans:

Be prepared, for you never know when the Lord will come.

Note: Sing 'Give me oil in my lamp' (JP).

Useful addresses

The Society for Promoting Christian Knowledge (SPCK)
Holy Trinity Church
Marylebone Road
London NW1 4DU

Catholic Fund for Overseas
    Development (CAFOD)
2 Romero Close
Stockwell Road
London SW9 9TY

Christian Aid
P.O. Box 100,
London,
SE1 7RT

Church Missionary Society (CMS)
157 Waterloo Road
London SE1 8UU

IBRA
Robert Denholm House
Nutfield
Redhill
Surrey RH1 4HW

The National Society
Church House
Great Smith Street
London SW1P 3NZ

Oxfam
274 Banbury Road
Oxford OX2 7DZ

South American Missionary
    Society (SAMS)
Allen Gardiner House
Pembury Road
Tunbridge Wells
Kent TN2 3QU

United Society for the
    Propagation of the Gospel
    (USPG)
157 Waterloo Road
London SE1 8XA

Amnesty International
British Section
99 Rosebery Avenue
London EC1R 4RE

One World Week
PO Box 100
London SE1 7RT